EQUITY MARKET DEVELOPMENT IN DEVELOPING COUNTRIES

BRYAN LORIN SUDWEEKS

D0075335

PRAEGER

New York
Westport, Connecticut
London

Library of Congress Cataloging-in-Publication Data

Sudweeks, Bryan Lorin.

 Equity market development in developing countries / Bryan Lorin
Sudweeks.

 p.   cm.

 Bibliography: p.

 Includes index.

 ISBN 0-275-92950-7 (alk. paper)

 1. Stocks—Developing countries. 2. Stock-exchange—Developing
countries. I. Title.

HG5993.S83   1989

332.64'09172'4—dc19   88-36532

Library of Congress Catalog Card Number: 88-36532
ISBN: 0-275-92950-7

First published in 1989

Praeger Publishers, One Madison Avenue, New York, NY 10010
A division of Greenwood Press, Inc.

Printed in the United States of America

The paper used in this book complies with the Permanent
Paper Standard issued by the National Information Standards
Organization (Z39.48--1984).

10 9 8 7 6 5 4 3 2 1

EQUITY MARKET DEVELOPMENT IN DEVELOPING COUNTRIES

Contents

Tables and Figures

TABLES

FIGURES

Acknowledgments

A book like this could not be completed without significant effort by many people. Although naming all contributors is not possible, certain individuals deserve mention.

The author expresses appreciation to Antoine W. van Agtmael, president of Emerging Markets Investors Corporation, for his insights into emerging markets and his unfailing belief that these markets are the wave of the future; Dr. Alex Anckonie III for his excellent ideas, comments, suggestions, and help on the original document and his untiring interest in international investment; Dr. Marta Oyhenart of George Washington University for her comments and practical ideas on the benefits of equity markets to developing countries; Peter Wall and Peter Tropper of the International Finance Corporation for their help on data gathering; Drs. Phillip Grub, Yoon Park, and William Handorf of George Washington University for their review and comments on various drafts; and my colleagues at Emerging Markets Investors Corporation, especially Michael Duffy and Josephine Jimenez, for their help and day-to-day contributions to the development of emerging capital markets. Most important, the author expresses thanks to his wife Anne and daughters Kimberly and Natalie for their support and love during this long-term project.

The views expressed in this book are entirely those of the author and do not in any way reflect the views of the Emerging Markets Investors Corporation or any other affiliated individual or institution.

EQUITY MARKET
DEVELOPMENT
IN
DEVELOPING
COUNTRIES

1

Introduction

Financial flows to developing countries (DCs) have changed dramatically in the last few years. Commercial and multilateral bankers, once eager to make loans to DCs, have held constant, curtailed, or completely stopped new loans. Regional U.S. banks, once heavy into developing country loans, have reached their self-determined "prudent" lending limits and are not expected to increase their exposure. The growth rate of international bank claims on developing countries has decreased substantially since 1979.

Sovereign and international bond markets have also declined in importance as another source of funds for many DCs. New issues by developing countries as a percentage of total issues has remained constant, albeit at a low level of 5 percent, with only five developing countries accounting for over two-thirds of the issues.

Many DCs have realized that the external capital markets are not the only, nor necessarily the best, source of funds for development or other purposes. International credit and markets, although enticing for certain periods of time, may not be in a country's best interests, because of repayment requirements, lack of flexibility, and increases in interest rates when a country's financial conditions deteriorate.

Private capital flows from many developing countries are also occurring. Efforts to halt these outflows through government regulation have not been effective. The exodus of "flight capital" has destabilized interest and exchange rates, reduced domestic investment, eroded the domestic tax base, and increased government and private borrowing abroad.

Efforts to increase the savings rate in DCs have not been successful. With rapid changes in government policy, inflation, and other

1

destabilizing factors, savings is being replaced by current consumption, investment in real assets (i.e., real estate and gold), and capital flight.

DC governments are also realizing the untapped potential of internal capital markets. Many are finding that capital flight is not a foregone conclusion but a predictable response to various political, economic, and other factors. Once thought to be gone forever, capital flight has been found to return once conditions and markets that offer attractive opportunities to domestic investors have been established. Moreover, whereas capital flight was once considered totally external to the developing country's actions, many officials are beginning to review their own policies and guidelines to see the effect they have on real returns, investor confidence, and capital flows.

Developing countries are also analyzing the effect of "real" rates of return on savings mobilization. They have found that savings increase when real rates of interest on investments are positive, not negative. Investors shift their savings from lower to higher return alternatives, based on their individual risk and return preferences. The view of individuals in developing countries as rational investors, not just unquestioning followers of government authority, is rapidly changing.

Other views are also changing. Whereas DCs once regarded foreign investment with disdain, now many countries are actively courting foreign portfolio and direct investment. Whereas countries once purchased technology outright, technology has become one of the bargaining chips in the negotiating process for investment. Whereas once the only concern was availability of funds, means and methods to raise capital for development are being evaluated with a more critical analysis of the repayment mechanisms, flexibility, and implications on control, foreign exchange, and development capabilities of the projects.

Parallel to these changing views by developing country governments has been the attention by economists, academicians, and country policy experts to endogenous sources of raising funds. This examination has led to considering domestic financial markets not only as a means of capital formation but also as a tool to promote economic development. With the study of financial markets, the quest for understanding the links between financial development and economic development has evolved.

Traditional economic and monetary theory has given financial development a very limited importance in comparison to other variables in the process of furthering economic development. Strategies for economic development have traditionally emphasized large foreign-aid transfers, capital inflows, or subsidies from other nations. Although well intended, these transfers have often been insufficient, ineffective, and sometimes damaging to the recipients' fundamental economic problems.

During the last 20 years, the results of previous policy actions and world economic conditions have forced changes in development theory. With the change to flexible exchange rates, the interdependence of world markets, the debt problems of developing countries, and the oil crises of 1973–1974, 1981–1982, and 1985–1986, financial development has taken on renewed importance. The relationship between money and physical capital is being reemphasized in a complete sense, as is the influence of monetary and fiscal policies on capital market development. With that relationship, investors and policy makers have gained a greater awareness of the potential contribution of a domestic securities market in developing countries.

PHILOSOPHY OF FINANCIAL MARKET BUILDING

If there was any doubt about the importance of domestic capital markets in ensuring balanced economic growth, the history of the 1980s to date must dispel it.[1] The chronic problems of country and corporate overindebtedness have brought home the dangers of combining too much short-term debt with too little long-term equity.

The causes of this situation are partially understandable. Past work on financial market building by many developing countries and organizations, such as the World Bank, emphasized development finance institutions (DFIs) and the banking system. Until recently, risk capital, financial markets, and nonbanking financial institutions were largely ignored. With the focus primarily on intermediation, little attention was paid to the possibilities of overintermediation, excessive debt to equity.

The varieties of market institutions and instruments are mentioned in the literature. However, the emphasis has been on the banking system and DFIs. Over time, the evolution of the bank-centered systems under government regulation have displayed major deficiencies. Past and current experiences have shown that most developing countries require greater variety in institutions and instruments than bank-centered financial systems allow. From one point of view, this could be considered a break with current policy. But from another vantage point, it is the next important step in the evolution of an efficient and stable financial system.

Objectives of a Financial System

Financial development work should respond to specific development objectives of individual countries. However, all financial systems
have general objectives. These are to contribute to faster, sustainable,
and socially equitable economic growth.[2] These can be achieved
through efficient intermediation (bringing together both investors and
borrowers), efficient allocation (allocating resources to their most
productive use), adequate savings mobilization (mobilizing savings
through financial instruments, rather than real assets), stability (absence
of financial crisis, effective term transformation, and adequate risk
capital), adequate accumulation of retirement funds (accumulating
sufficient retirement funds for investors' nonproductive years), and social
equity through broad access (allowing all members of society an
opportunity to access the financial markets). An efficient and stable
financial system will involve the creation of many different types of
financial institutions and instruments. This ensures a reasonable
distribution of savings among short-term (deposit-type or money market)
instruments, long-term debt instruments (bonds), and risk capital (stocks
and related instruments) to meet the overall financing needs of the
economy.

Two areas that have not received adequate attention to date are the
importance of translating the concept of a competitive market into
institutional reality and the historical discrimination in the treatment of
various financial instruments and institutions. These areas have led to
many lopsided financial systems in developing countries, where the
vested interests of large institutions (banks) dominate the financial system
to such an extent that they can bar new institutions despite their own lack
of efficiency.

Intrasectoral Competition versus Intersectoral Competition

In order to achieve its objectives, the financial system must be
efficient and solvent. Efficiency is best promoted by competition,
hampered by as few market imperfections as possible. All segments of
the financial system will not have the same degree of competition.
Because of institutional considerations (solvency and economies of
scale), however, dilemmas arise when the actual conditions fall short of
competitive characteristics.

In most developing countries, bank-centered financial systems, the commercial and deposit-taking banks, attempt to limit competition in the interest of institutional stability or solvency. In fact, licensing requirements for the opening of commercial banks are numerous. In particular, capital requirements tend to be high, representing the need for solvency, whereas public policy discourages other entrants, resulting in fewer financial institutions.

But solvency and efficiency may be at odds. The promotion of fewer and bigger units is a countercompetitive policy, and the result is large, powerful institutions. Thus market signals may represent not the interaction of a wide range of forces, but simply the influence of a few large institutions. This causes a contradiction in promoting bank-centered financial systems; operational considerations tilt policy toward fewer and larger units, which decreases competition and reduces the pressures for efficiency. The system that emerges has a few powerful institutions and little competition, a situation found today in many developing countries. Trying to encourage competition in a bank-centered financial system entails trying to maintain competition among the few, the central problem that large institutions try to avoid. Perhaps a better way would be to regulate financial institutions to attempt to force greater efficiency. Although in theory this appears credible, in reality large institutions have powerful vested interests and typically resist such pressures quite effectively.

Another problem lies in the nature of competition in a bank-centered market. Competition itself does not result in a stable equilibrium market condition. While the strong survive, the weak and inefficient are eliminated, again resulting in a few large institutions.

Promoting competition from within the banking system may be a difficult undertaking, as has been experienced by many developing countries. But increasing the available instruments in which the public can invest may be a solution to this problem.

Here, capital and money markets play a major role. The lower capital requirements and the greater importance of entrepreneurship relative to capital in nonbank financial institutions mean that two characteristics of the market are becoming visible — greater number of participants and greater ease of entry. Thus, in achieving efficiency through competition, the focus on competition within the banking sector should be changed to competition within the financial system, i.e., with deposit-taking institutions on the one hand and financial markets and nonbank financial institutions on the other. Public authorities would continue to promote safety solvency, and, possibly, economies of scale in the banking sector through high-capitalization, large-unit policies while encouraging competition from the money and capital markets, institutional investors (insurance companies and pension funds), and specialized, quasi-banking nonfinancial institutions (leasing, venture capital, and check discounting). Only a few countries have pursued these policies consciously and systematically (the United States, Canada, Japan, Korea, and Brazil). In these cases, the results have been supportive of healthy and viable financial markets.

Would nationalized banks promote efficiency in developing countries? In India after nationalization, the profitability of the banking system deteriorated, in large part, because of loan overdues, overstaffing, and low efficiency due to outdated procedures and banking technology. The results in other DCs have been similar.

Would competition between nationalized banks increase efficiency? The results in Mexico showed that when the banks were nationalized, deposit taking in real terms fell while the proportion of bank loans going to the public sector increased significantly, thus crowding out the private-sector investments. Moreover, the two largest banks in Mexico account for about half the assets of the commercial banking system.

But Mexico experienced something different. The Mexican Central Bank encouraged a company paper market either among buyers and sellers or through securities dealers. Indications were that these and other nonbank financial institutions were allowed to keep the nationalized banks competitive. This intersectoral competition, not only between different institutions but also in the available financial instruments, is an example of the type of competition necessary for the development of a balanced financial system in developing countries.

Equity in Fund Mobilization

The second principle that has not yet received attention is the necessity of equity in fund mobilization. There are various sectors in the financial system consisting of different types of institutions (deposit and nondeposit) and oriented toward different purposes (debt or equity) and time horizons (long-term or short-term), but there is only one pool of savings. Savers should be able to place their funds on the basis of their investment objectives and time horizons. Governments affect savings behavior through various fiscal, monetary, and economic policies. In theory, government-induced influences (if there are any) that operate on savings behavior should be the result of carefully formulated public policies aimed at clear public-interest objectives (promotion of equity ownership, diffusion of corporate shareholding, and encouragement of long-term financial instruments). Ideally, the allocative influence should be zero, but this is unlikely to prevail. Governments should attempt to minimize distortions originating from haphazard influences in order to achieve some equity in the mobilization and management of savings.

The principal allocative influences (or distortions) come from fiscal, monetary, and economic policies. Fiscal policies have been widely identified as affecting the relative attractiveness of debt and equity instruments. Monetary policy impinges more on the relative advantages as between deposit and nondeposit instruments, between bank and nonbank operations. Economic policies, at least their results, tend to affect the attractiveness of various instruments in times of economic growth versus times of recession. In a balanced financial system, these allocative influences should be at a minimum. Allocative influences are not necessarily bad. These same influences can be useful development tools aiding the evolution of the financial system necessary to achieve specific goals of developing countries.

WHY EQUITY MARKETS?

The previous discussion shows the need for both intrasectoral competition and intersectoral competition in most financial systems. Moreover, the addition of other instruments has beneficial effects on the savings mobilization and efficient allocation of assets. The question, "Why equity markets?" must be asked.

Equity markets are important because they allow competition between various instruments of a bank-centered financial system and the nonbank financial intermediaries. They also allow risk sharing on an individual basis, without a government guarantee; offer instruments that do not suffer from a cash-flow mismatch; and encourage the development of other financial markets.

Equity markets allow competition between various instruments of the bank and nonbank financial system based on each investor's risk, return, and time considerations. In a bank-centered financial system, the options for lenders and borrowers are limited. Investors are constrained to safe but low, often negative rates of return in the regulated financial markets or to the higher, riskier rates of return in the unregulated markets. Lenders are constrained to the high rates of interest charged by banks or are constrained by the amount of internally generated funds or available credit on the high-risk unregulated markets.

Equity markets have no mandated ceiling on returns. They offer an alternative to safe but low, often negative real returns in developing countries. Investors have a greater range of risk and return opportunities than in the bank or unregulated financial markets. Equity markets allow greater matching of risk and return characteristics of lenders and borrowers. Moreover, when equity returns do not compensate for the risk, investors have the option to switch to less risky assets with more stable returns or to the safe deposit-type assets of the bank financial institutions.

Equity markets allow risk sharing, which is not government guaranteed. Most commercial bank loans to developng countries have involved explicit or implicit government guarantees. Whereas the funds were earmarked for a specific project or program, their repayment was not contingent on that project's outcome but was borne by the guarantor, the government. This means that risks inherent in projects or strategies were shifted to the lender only through government default, a very costly alternative. Moreover, for private-sector projects, it exposed the government to mistakes and bad management by removing the project from the discipline of the financial markets. When a developing country finances an investment project by incurring debt, it implicitly accepts the risks of the activity being financed. Because the lender has little stake in the success of the project, there is little motivation to intervene in its design or management. Equity markets returns are not guaranteed by the government. Expected returns are based solely on the performance of the company itself, not on the government guarantees. Moreover, the investor is motivated by the results of the company because the return is directly related to company performance.

Equity markets do not suffer from cash-flow mismatch. Most developing countries and companies experience fluctuations in revenue because of world economic cycles, shifts in the terms of trade, and domestic political and economic events. Ideally, by borrowing in times of low income and repaying debt in times of high income, international finance should help smooth national consumption and company expenditures over time. However, if a country or firm already has substantial obligations, it may have difficulty borrowing more, and the need to service its existing debt may intensify the fluctuations in the underlying level of income. Thus, in response to various shocks in the world economy, developing countries and firms may need to borrow more, but, because of an already high debt-service burden, international and domestic financial organizations may not be willing to incur additional risk.

These problems are not present in equity markets. When an investor purchases equity, no loan must be repaid. In times of prosperity, the dividends usually increase as a result of better corporate profitability. Likewise, in times of austerity, dividends are often reduced to retain funds needed by the company.

Finally, equity markets encourage the development of other financial markets. General obligation bank lending inhibits the development of the local capital markets. Where monopoly power exists, there is little incentive to develop markets that would limit, or even eliminate, that monopoly power. Established banks tend to protect their markets, hindering the development of additional markets. Moreover, considerable effort is often required to convince established banks to lessen their market dominance and encourage the development of additional financial markets.

Equity markets do not suffer from this problem. The establishment of an equity market establishes the necessary groundwork for bond and other financial markets. As the markets develop, the liquidity and risk reduction needs of corporations and government may also lead to the development of other markets dealing in other financial instruments, such as futures and options to meet the additional needs of market participants.

ASSUMPTIONS OF EQUITY MARKET DEVELOPMENT

One of the assumptions of equity market development is that investors and borrowers in developing countries are rational investors. From this assumption come various statements: investors prefer higher returns to lower returns, lower risks to higher risks, greater disclosure of information to less disclosure, and more stable cash flows to less stable cash flows. Likewise, borrowers prefer lower borrowing rates to higher rates, more control over operations to less control, flexible payback mechanisms to more rigid methods, less information disclosure to more information disclosure, and greater cash flows in the present versus the future. This assumption is consistent with the observed pattern in developed countries.

Various sectors in the financial system are oriented toward different institutions, purposes, and time horizons. Various individuals and institutions, the government being a major player, compete for those funds. However, there is only one pool of savings. Governments have the ability to print more money, but the effect of a too-rapid expansion in the money supply may result in inflation in the long run. Governments have the ability to require savers to invest in government securities. But this may lead to exclusion of the private sector, capital flight, and reduced economic growth. Governments have the ability and responsibility to pass and enforce regulations to support various goals. However, they cannot regulate the results of many of those same policies. Likewise, private companies may issue equity, but if the expected return is not sufficient given the underlying risk, they may find investors unwilling to commit their funds. Private companies may issue bonds, but if a company lacks credibility, investors may require a much higher interest rate, increasing the financial costs of the company. Some of the problems faced by developing countries, such as capital flight, shallow financial systems, and large debt burdens, are to a degree the result of well-meaning but improper domestic legislation, regulation, or corporate strategy. Likewise, to the extent that proper legislation has been established, the development of financial markets in developing countries is also apparent. Comparative analysis of different developing countries shows that many of the problems in DCs can be eliminated or reduced through correct and timely government and private action based on proper policy measures.

One of the reasons for the more rapid development of the equity markets in certain developing countries has been the proper understanding and implementation of the cause and effect relationships of different government policies on financial markets. Governments that enact legislation based on both the cause and effect relationships are much more likely than those governments that fail to determine possible results of various legislation to achieve a specific desired outcome. This book presents a general framework to allow the understanding of various actions on the evolution of equity markets in developing countries.

PURPOSE AND ORGANIZATION OF THE BOOK

The purpose of this book is to give a greater perspective to equity market development programs in developing countries by considering important factors. Three factors are critical:

Equity market development must be part of an overall financial system development program to achieve the goals and objectives of each country. The goal is not to develop an equity market but to develop a balanced financial system in order to achieve specific country goals and objectives, of which an equity market is a part.

Equity market development is generally a private-sector activity, with government having a strong supporting role. As such, there must be continual private-sector dialogue in all stages of development.

Equity market development is a very difficult, time-consuming, complex, and yet somewhat predictable process. It cannot be stopped at will because major factors are public confidence and long-term corporate profitability. It must be implemented with caution and skill, with an emphasis toward the assumptions of each action and the implications on both the private and public sectors.

This book is organized as follows. Chapter 1 gives the historical background of funding in developing countries. It shows that current development thinking must be pushed to the next frontier and that a broader range of financial instruments is necessary in developing countries.

Chapter 2 shows the logical evolution of ideas behind the theory of financial and economic development and that equity markets are the next step for many developing countries. It also discusses that, with the globalization of markets and modern portfolio theory, these DC markets should be of interest to international investors. Finally, it relates that for firms to remain competitive internationally, they can reduce their cost of capital by diversifying their investor base.

Chapter 3 reviews the benefits and costs of equity markets within a balanced financial system. Governments and private sector individuals must be aware of the benefits of equity markets, to ensure they outweigh the costs. Equity markets are not a panacea for all problems; however, few viable alternatives can achieve the same objectives.

Chapter 4 presents general conditions that are beneficial to the development of an equity market. Equity market development is a difficult, but generally predictable, undertaking. Actions that maintain public confidence and the short- and long-term value of an equity certificate (company profitability) will contribute to the development of the market.

Chapter 5 discusses measures used by DCs to encourage the supply of shares. Without an adequate supply of shares, too many people chasing too few stocks causes many problems. In developing countries, encouraging the supply and demand for shares must be addressed simultaneously.

Chapter 6 reviews measures used by DCs to encourage the demand for shares. Again, maintaining public confidence in equity markets and ensuring long-term profitability and viability of firms are critical.

Chapter 7 discusses portfolio implications of investing in DCs, including risk, return, and correlations, to the international portfolio investor. In addition, it discusses intermediary steps used by developing countries to internationalize the markets, without some of the perceived problems of full equity market liberalization.

Chapter 8 presents suggestions for an equity market development as part of a complete financial development program. In order to minimize future problems, instead of being the last stage of a financial development program, equity markets must be planned and various issues resolved in all stages of development.

Chapter 9 presents case studies of Brazil, India, and Korea and shows how various public and private policy decisions affected the development of the markets. The three major points of this book, that equity market development must be part of an overall financial system development program, that it must be private sector oriented, and that it is a complex and difficult, but somewhat predictable, undertaking, are readily apparent.

Finally, Chapter 10 presents the conclusions of the book.

Before continuing, some important terms must be defined. For the purpose of this book, financial development will be defined as the evolution of the financial structure within a country. This structure includes institutions, instruments, and activities brought about by intervention or natural consequences.[3] Edward Shaw coined the term "financial deepening" to refer to financial development, this positive evolution of financial structure over time.[4] There is no current, universally accepted definition for financial development.

Economic development is defined as the improvement in the economic situation of a country resulting from either natural evolution or intervention. It is usually measured by GNP per capita or some other form of variable: growth rates, increases in disposable income, or savings although more complete measures have been developed.

Financial structure refers to those institutions, legal systems, information systems, and public- and private-sector expertise essential to successful operation of securities markets and that maintain high levels of investor confidence.

Securities markets refer to the markets for debt and equity instruments with the accompanying financial structure required for successful operation (i.e., institutions, clearing and control mechanisms, information, legal and regulatory systems, and necessary public- and private-sector expertise essential to successful operation and investor confidence). Securities markets are divided into three major classifications: the primary market, which includes the initial sale/underwriting of securities; the secondary market, where seasoned issues are traded; and the third market, which trades listed securities off exchanges. Other classifications exist, such as the grey market for Eurobonds, but these are beyond the scope of this book.

Securities, or securities instruments, refer to the more traditional debt and equity issues used to develop capital and transfer funds. These include bonds, stocks, and other money market instruments, including recent instruments that allow hedging and speculation in securities and commodity markets, such as options, futures, and swaps.

Securities markets in many countries can be further divided into two separate markets, the money market and the capital market. The money market is a wholesale market for high-quality, short-term debt instruments. The money market allows participants an opportunity to adjust liquidity.

The capital market is composed of bonds, stocks and other instruments comprising the medium- to long-term maturities. Capital markets facilitate real wealth creation. The distinction between money and capital markets has been gradually narrowing in the past few years.

Finally, capital can be divided into two areas, equity and long-term debt. Equity refers to the markets for common and preferred stock of foreign, private, and quasi-government corporations or institutions.[5] The bond market refers to long-term debt instruments used for raising funds. Hybrid instruments exist, but the distinction between the two markets is maintained for the purpose of this book.

NOTES

1. The ideas and concepts of this section are largely a summary of Benito Legarda, "Philosophy of Financial Market Building," International Finance Corporation Discussion Paper, August 1986, and comments by Antoine W. van Agtmael.

2. Legarda, "Philosophy," 2.

3. Raymond Goldsmith, *Financial Structure and Development* (New Haven: Yale University Press, 1969), and Kahanya Gupta, *Finance and Economic Growth in Developing Countries* (London: Croom Helm, 1984).

4. Edward S. Shaw, *Financial Deepening in Economic Development* (New York: Oxford University Press, 1973).

5. In reality, there are many different types of equity markets. Because land, cars, and jewelry are also considered equity and because these assets can be bought and sold, they also could be considered types of equity markets. However, generally these assets are very illiquid. Equity markets in this book are limited to the regulated markets for financial instruments, i.e., common and preferred stock.

2

Theory Behind the Development of Equity Markets

The financial literature in developed countries discusses quite thoroughly the process and theory of financial markets. However, little attention has been given financial markets in developing countries. This next section discusses four major areas relating to the evolution of equity markets in developing countries: namely, financial and economic development theory, modern portfolio theory, and internationalization of the cost of capital. The fourth area discusses the academic literature on securities markets in developing countries.

FINANCIAL AND ECONOMIC DEVELOPMENT THEORY

The study of the role of money and finance in economic development has been a fairly recent phenomenon. Schumpeter was among the first to study the importance of financial development, financial intermediaries, with economic development.[1] He regarded banks and entrepreneurship as two key agents of development and discussed the importance of money capital in fostering development.

Keynes gave some importance to the role of financial development by relating equilibrium in the money markets to general equilibrium in the economy.[2] However, the Keynesians, in using the static equilibrium model, did not give importance to the study of imperfect or underdeveloped financial markets.

The neoclassicists, as did the Keynesians, treated money and finance as insignificant or neutral over all countries. However, in the early 1950s, economists began examining money and finance from different perspectives, with varying degrees of emphasis and success. Not until the early 1970s did economists start to extend the theoretical analysis to developing countries.

Beginning with the seminal works by McKinnon and Shaw, there began active research into the importance of financial development in the context of economic development, especially regarding developing countries.[3] Two views have arisen from these works. The financial repressionist view considers low real interest rates, caused by arbitrarily set ceilings on nominal interest rates and high and variable inflation rates, to be major impediments to financial deepening, capital formation and growth. The financial structuralist or financial deepening view maintains a widespread network of financial institutions have a beneficial effect on the saving investment processes, and hence, on growth.

From the financial repression concept emerged the theory of financial liberalization. This theory states that liberalization of the financial sector from interest rate ceilings and other restrictions facilitates economic development and growth because higher interest rates lead to both increased savings and greater efficiency of capital allocation.

Moving theory even further, other economists considered that financial liberalization theory, although important, was nonetheless incomplete. Whereas theory states the importance of eliminating interest rate ceilings and fostering competition among banks, Cho argued that it failed to take into account internal constraints on the credit markets, such as imperfect information. Moreover, it has also failed to note the oligopolistic and cartelized banking systems found in most DCs. Most important, theory thus far has neglected the potential role of equity markets for efficient capital allocation and risk sharing in a liberalized financial environment.[4]

This section will discuss five major areas of financial and economic development theory: the neoclassical model, financial repression, financial deepening, financial liberalization, and financial liberalization with equity markets.

The Neoclassical Model

One of the first and major theories of economic development that incorporated finance and money as an input was the neoclassical model. It was designed for mature economies with well-functioning capital markets. However, in most DCs this is not the case. As such, many of the explicit or implicit assumptions are not valid. There are four neoclassical assumptions of significance to securities markets:

Capital markets operate perfectly and costlessly to equate returns on all real and financial assets (other than money) with a single (risk adjusted) rate of interest, the nominal rate that reflects expected inflation accurately.

Inputs (including capital) and outputs are perfectly divisible with constant returns to scale in the prototype enterprise. An individual firm can be considered a miniature replica of the aggregate production function, with identical technology and prices in commodity and factor markets.

There is an important transactions demand for money in avoiding the need for the well-known double coincidence of wants. Money, however, plays no direct role in capital accumulation, per se, because the first assumption above implies a perfect market in physical capital and interest-bearing claims on it.

Real money balances are virtually socially costless to produce for satisfying this transactions motive. Hence, money can be thought of as the outside fiat type being issued by the government for current services, and there is no meaningful distinction between currency and deposits.[5]

As can be seen, many of the important assumptions are not valid in the context of a developing country. The neoclassical model was intended for a very specific set of assumptions, which do not transfer well to poor, fragmented economies, even over a fairly long time horizon in which to select asset portfolios. Moreover, it omits issues of particular importance to less-developed countries and contains many unfortunate biases.

The neoclassicists, Schumpeter, and Keynes dealt with developing countries in terms of "market imperfections." However, in recent years another group of economists have addressed the connection between financial market imperfections and economic growth.

Financial Repression

McKinnon was one of the first to state that the previously used monetary and Keynesian policies for developing countries had not worked well. He established another theory, a financial repressionist theory, and discussed its implications for country policy. The centerpiece of the theory is the domestic capital market within each developing country and the way in which that market's operations are influenced by monetary and fiscal policies. Money and finance, as governed by the banking system, are given a degree of importance much greater than that accorded by most authors concerned with development.

McKinnon argued that acceptable theories of monetarism and financial processes, whether Keynesian or monetarist, could not explain the dominance of real money balances in the operation of capital markets in poor countries. Both of these prevailing theories assume that capital markets are essentially perfect, with a single governing rate of interest or a term structure of interest rates, whereas in underdeveloped countries there is overwhelming fragmentation in real rates of interest. As a result, both theories treat real money balances and physical capital as substitutes for each other although a relation of "complementarity" better explains the data in certain critical circumstances over certain time frames. For the undeveloped economy, the demand for real cash balances and the demand for physical capital are highly complementary in private asset portfolios, in contrast to prevailing theory, where a substitution relationship is dominant.

McKinnon's basic thesis of complementarity between money and capital implies that large and fast-growing real cash balances contribute to rapid growth in investment and in aggregate output. Furthermore, for official policies to make a critical difference in the real size of the monetary system, the private sector must be sensitive to the real interest rates chosen for deposits and loans. Low, possibly negative, real lending and deposit interest rates shrink real cash balances.[6] Correspondingly, measures taken to relieve this financial repression expand real cash balances and lead to increased saving and investment.

Financial Deepening

Shaw and McKinnon had similar ideas, yet Shaw took a different approach to the relationship between money and capital. Instead of the complementarity idea, Shaw maintained that expanded financial intermediation between savers and investors resulting from financial liberalization increased incentives to save and invest and increased the efficiency of savings. Financial intermediaries raise real returns to savers and lower costs to borrowers by accommodating liquidity preference, increasing operational efficiency, achieving economies of scale, and lowering information costs.[7] Financial intermediation is repressed or suboptimal when administered rates of interest are set below the equilibrium rate. When interest rates are used as rationing devices, financial intermediaries can use their expertise to allocate the investable funds in the most efficient manner.

Shaw maintained, in contrast to McKinnon, that real yields on all forms of wealth, including money, have a positive effect on domestic savings. Complementarity is not valid as investors are not constrained to self-finance as McKinnon proposes. Where institutional credit is unavailable, noninstitutional markets invariably occur (kerb markets, moneylenders, and cooperatives).

Although Shaw explicitly addresses the question of "imperfect financial markets," his policy recommendations seem to imply that DC markets are perfect in disseminating information. However, in developing countries there are still many barriers to information dissemination, such as poor communication infrastructure, lack of trained financial and accounting personnel, and cultural backgrounds not conducive to information disclosure.

Financial Liberalization

From the works of McKinnon and Shaw has risen the theory of financial liberalization. This theory states that liberalization of the financial sector from interest rate ceilings and other restrictions facilitates economic development and growth because higher interest rates lead to both increased savings and greater efficiency of capital allocation.

In spite of the perceived benefits of financial liberalization, many countries still hesitate to liberalize their financial systems. Moreover many countries, even industrial countries (for example, Japan) have hesitated to liberalize their financial markets, and others have returned to financial repression after limited periods of liberalization attempts (for example, Korea and Argentina). The question of "Why?" must be asked. Cho argues that full-scale liberalization of the banking sector would not achieve efficient capital allocation in the absence of a well-functioning equity market and that substantial development of an equity market is a necessary condition for complete financial liberalization.[8]

Financial Liberalization with Equity Markets

Financial liberalization theory, although important, is incomplete. Whereas theory states the importance of eliminating interest rate ceilings and fostering competition among banks, it has failed to consider internal constraints such as imperfect information, on the credit markets. Moreover, it has also failed to note the oligopolistic and cartelized banking systems found in most DCs. Theory thus far has neglected the potential role of equity markets for efficient capital allocation and risk sharing in a liberalized financial environment.

There are two possible constraints on credit markets where differential interest rates are set according to borrowers' characteristics. The first is the legal or institutional constraint, such as interest rate ceilings, which impinge on the setting of differential interest rates. The second constraint arises because of the costs (especially information costs) of distinguishing between the risk characteristics of different customers, particularly new customers. Even if banks are liberalized (the elimination of the institutional constraint), the improvement in the efficiency of capital allocation is not assured if the information constraints are very strong.

Although the financial liberalization literature has placed emphasis on the elimination of external constraints, it has largely neglected the internal constraints. These constraints can be a significant barrier to efficient credit allocation even when external constraints, such as interest rate ceilings, are eliminated. Most of the credit rationing literature has modeled these internal constraints to explain rationing in competitive credit markets.[9] Two authors who discuss the question of efficiency of credit rationing are Stiglitz and Weiss.[10] They suggest that given several groups of borrowers, imperfect information results in some being excluded from the credit market, although the expected returns of the projects may be higher than those that get credit. Moreover, they also suggest that the profitability of banks may not be an increasing function of the interest rates it charges borrowers. First, the safe borrowers, those the bank is most interested in and would most profitably lend to, may be deterred because of the high cost of capital (the adverse selection effect). Second, when interest rates are high, borrowers tend to favor riskier projects with higher probability of default (the incentive effect). If the project turns out as expected, the borrowers make profit of the return less the interest expense, while the bank makes only the interest rate, regardless of the extent the return exceeds the rate of interest. Likewise, if the return is not as the borrower expected, the borrower may simply lose the fixed amount of collateral, if any, while the bank suffers the whole loss. Therefore, the expected profit to the borrower increases with the riskiness of the project whereas the expected profit of the bank decreases with the riskiness of the project when the total return on investment and interest rate are held constant.

Because of imperfect information, to achieve full efficiency of capital allocation in a liberalized financial system, the development of an equity market is necessary. Equity capital can finance the risky, productive borrowers for whom asymmetric information is lacking while banks concentrate on the other well-established, safe borrowers.

The most efficient capital allocation is achieved by liberalizing the financial markets. However, if the financial markets are composed only of debt-financing institutions, such as banks, the market does not achieve efficient allocation of capital because of shortcomings of debt finance in the presence of asymmetric information.

Cho and others emphasize the importance of financial liberalization, with the important caveat of the necessity of a domestic equity market to finance the riskier projects.

The above authors discuss the importance of equity markets in the context of economic development theory. But equity markets allow other important benefits. These include greater opportunities for diversification, both domestically and internationally, as well as the possibility of increased market efficiency. Diversification and efficiency are two important areas of modern portfolio theory.

MODERN PORTFOLIO THEORY

Another area of theory important to equity markets is the demand for domestic securities. This demand could take many forms: purchases of securities on the domestic exchange, sales of domestic shares on foreign exchanges, or sales of depository receipts on foreign exchanges. Demand for emerging market securities is partially a result of the possible decrease in risk and increase in return resulting from international diversification, an area of modern portfolio theory.[11] In addition to international diversification, this section discusses efficient markets as well as the considered set and efficient frontiers.

International Diversification

Modern portfolio theory discusses the relationship of return and risk in a given portfolio of financial assets. To analyze a given portfolio, three estimates for every security must be considered: the expected return, the variance of returns, and the covariances between that security and all other securities. The expected return on a portfolio is simply a weighted average of the expected returns on the individual assets (see Table 2.1).[12] Expected returns of individual securities can be estimated in many different ways. Returns can be estimated using historical data and various types of forecasting techniques. If the historical data are accurate, and future conditions will be similar to past conditions, historical data may be the best estimate. However, if the market is changing, often subjective estimates by analysts expert in the market may be better estimates.

The variance of a portfolio (or risk) is more difficult to determine. The variance of a portfolio is the expected value of the squared deviations of the returns of the combined assets in the portfolio from the mean return on the portfolio. The use of the variance as a measure of dispersion of returns implicitly assumes that the effect of variability is best captured by the square of the difference between the return and the expectation. Thus, a return twice as far removed from the expectation is four times as important in measuring the impact of the variability of the return. A more compact version of the equation is found in Table 2.1. The term "risk" could be substituted for dispersion of returns around the expected value.

The second set of terms in the variance of a portfolio is the covariance or measure of how the returns on assets move together. The covariance

TABLE 2.1
Portfolio Mathematical Formulas

$$E(r_{Port}) = \sum_{i=1}^{n} x_i E(r_i)$$

$E(r)$ = Expected return
Port = portfolio
i,j = financial assets
x = percentage of the ith asset in the portfolio
n = number of assets in the portfolio
r = return

$$Var(r_{Port}) = \sum_{i=1}^{n} \sum_{j=1}^{n} x_i x_j \, cov(i,j)$$

$$Cov(r_i, r_j) = \sum_{i=1}^{n} \sum_{j=1}^{n} (r_i - E(r_i)) * (r_j - E(r_j)) * p(r_i, r_j)$$

Cov = covariance
p = joint probability that $x(i)$ and $x(j)$ take on the values simultaneously

of two assets in a portfolio is the return of one asset less the expected return, times the return of the second asset less its expected return, all multiplied by the joint probability that the two assets will take on the values simultaneously (see formula, Table 2.1). For a portfolio with a large number of assets, the variance would include the covariance between each asset and all other assets in the portfolio.

This variance is important in any given market in that by increasing the number of assets in a portfolio, the individual risk of assets can be diversified away (the diversifiable portion), but the contribution to the total risk caused by the covariance terms cannot be diversified away (the nondiversifiable portion). That is, as the number of assets in a portfolio increases, the variance is reduced until it approaches the average covariance between all stocks in the portfolio.

Within any given market and with a large portfolio, the variance of a portfolio can be reduced until it approaches the average covariance between all securities. International diversification describes how the correlation of securities from different countries (covariance of securities within one country with securities of another country divided by the product of the standard deviations of each security) is usually less than the correlation between securities of a single country. [13] Hence, including foreign securities in a portfolio may have the effect of reducing the covariance terms, reducing the nondiversifiable risk. [14] Hence, because of the differences in covariances between countries, there should be a demand for emerging country stocks by foreign investors, assuming the developing stocks and or stock markets meet all other investor requirements, for example, adequate yield, liquidity, and safety.

In addition, large portfolios in developing countries, such as pension fund portfolios, should operate at an improved return-to-risk ratio if such portfolios were allowed to consider some fraction of foreign financial assets in their portfolio selection considered set.

Efficient Markets Theory

Another area of concern to emerging securities markets is the concept of efficient markets. This concept, in financial theory, refers to the assumption that security prices reflect all available information. [15] Markets are said to be efficient if security prices are a reflection of all available information that investors consider relevant to their decisions to buy, sell, or hold a security.

Efficient market theory is based on certain key assumptions about the institutional environment: the market is composed of numerous individual and institutional participants; the participants have access to sufficient funds to affect security prices; transactions costs are low, which refers to both brokerage commissions and the spread between bid and offer prices; and a consensus judgment exists about the implications of available information for individual security prices.

These assumptions have been extremely stringent requirements for many economic theories past and present. Although developing country securities markets may not be efficient in all areas, it is hoped that over time and with correct government regulation the efficiency of the markets will improve.

The efficient market hypothesis has been divided into three categories, each dealing with a different type of information. The weak-form test of efficient markets checks whether all available historical information is contained in the current securities price. The semi-strong form tests whether all publicly available information is fully reflected in current stock prices. Finally, the strong-form tests whether all information, public or private, is fully reflected in security prices and whether any investor can make an excess profit (profits from insider information) using this information. Efficient market tests are also concerned with the speed at which information is assimilated into securities prices. If the markets are price inefficient, regardless of form, this indicates possibilities for excess return, profit above an expected return in a market where prices reflect all available information.

Efficient markets are an important aspect of developing capital markets. When prices in the market are artificially affected in any form, where governments regulate the price of securities in a stock market or where stock prices are manipulated by different groups, the market is not efficient. Moreover, where markets are not efficient, those with the ability and capability will make excess returns while risk-averse investors will not invest funds unless the expected risk and return characteristics of the market are still greater than alternative forms of investment. Alternative investments include official forms, such as banks deposits, government securities, or postal savings deposits; unofficial forms, such as curb markets or capital flight; or investment or consumption forms, such as increased inventories or purchases of goods, real estate, or gold. Where markets are not efficient, investors do not have confidence in a fair market and are reluctant to invest their savings. Investor confidence in the market is an important precursor and requirement to securities market growth and development.[16]

Through the efforts of many researchers, efficiency in the weak-form and semi-strong form test have been established for the U.S. securities market. In a comprehensive analysis of the European equity markets, Hawawini gives an extensive overview of the work done in European countries, including Austria, Belgium, Denmark, Finland, France, Germany, Greece, Italy, Netherlands, Norway, Sweden, and the United Kingdom.[17] He lists 53 articles that test weak-form efficiency. His results are that, in general, most of the markets are weak-form efficient, although some of the smaller markets are informationally inefficient. In the semi-strong form tests, he lists 33 event studies, the majority of which were performed on the larger markets. The results were that generally the markets were consistent with market efficiency in the semi-strong form. Many of the markets of the European countries, because of their relative thinness, can be considered emerging markets. In addition to these emerging markets, there have been a few scattered tests of efficiency in other developing countries.

Most of the work done in emerging markets has been to test the weak-form of the efficient markets hypothesis. In a test of the Korean market, Anckonie and Chi found that companies in the international trade or competitive industries tended to be more efficient (in the sense of absence of significant serial correlations) than those in other industries.[18] In a test of the Kuwaiti market, Gandhi, Saunders, and Woodward found the market also with inefficiencies in price determination (serial correlation), although there was excellent potential for international diversification.[19] In a study of the Mexican Stock Market, Solis and Usobiaga found first and second order autocorrelations not significantly different from zero, indicating possible efficiency, assuming higher orders of autocorrelation were not present.[20] In a test of the Kuala Lumpur and Singapore Stock Markets, Laurence found that in the actively traded stocks of the two exchanges, serial correlation coefficients, runs tests, and distributional statistics show that those markets are relatively weak-form efficient.[21]

In a test of emerging markets, Errunza and Losq analyzed the most liquid stocks on the exchanges of Argentina, Brazil, Chile, Greece, India, Jordan, Korea, Mexico, Thailand, and Zimbabwe for the period from December 1975 to April 1981.[22] The stocks analyzed, although not as efficient as major developing country markets, were found comparable to the smaller European markets in weak-form efficiency. Finally, in a more recent test, Sudweeks tested the same countries with actual stocks from developing countries (versus market indices). Using more powerful autoregressive and runs tests, he found DC stocks prices generally weak-form efficient and comparable to smaller European stock exchanges.[23] Analysis of the current efficiency tests done on developing countries suggests that the most actively traded stocks on the exchanges tend toward weak-form efficiency.

Considered Set and Efficient Frontiers

Another area of portfolio theory of concern to emerging markets is the "considered set" of assets in the portfolio. The considered set is the group of possible assets considered for inclusion in the investor's portfolio.

One could consider and plot the set of all risky assets and combinations of assets in a diagram with the horizontal axis being standard deviation of expected return and the vertical axis being the expected rate of return. By two assumptions, one could eliminate a major part of the assets from consideration. Those assumptions are that a single portfolio offers a greater return for the same risk and that a single portfolio offers a lower risk for the same return. All other portfolios could be safely ignored.

What we have described is called the efficient frontier. It is a plot of possible relationships between expected return and standard deviation of return for all assets in the portfolio at various levels of risk and return. The efficient frontier is a function of the currency with which the portfolio performance is evaluated, the numeraire currency. Portfolios evaluated from the U.S. Dollar point of view will have a different efficient frontier than the same portfolio evaluated from the Japanese yen or Korean won point of view.

Standard portfolio theory also discusses elimination of the constraints of short sales, constraints that place limits on the fraction of a portfolio that may be invested in a single asset and also on the ability to lend and borrow at a riskless rate. What is important is that by eliminating constraints, or by increasing the considered set, the efficient frontier may be pushed up and to the right, i.e., creating greater opportunities for higher return and lower risk.

This has importance to securities markets in developing countries in that the opportunities for investment in a developing country without a securities market are limited to banks and domestic moneylenders. However, as the securities market is developed, considered set for local investors increases, thereby allowing the efficient frontier to move up and to the right, giving opportunities for greater returns. As the return increases and risk decreases, funds will be transferred from lesser- to higher-return assets. Moreover, most institutional investors consider assets only from the developed countries in their portfolios. The addition of assets from developing countries will have the same effect of increasing the considered set and pushing the efficient frontier up and to the right, giving opportunities for higher return.

Most of the discussion thus far has been limited to the investors' or the developing country governments' point of view. But equity markets can have important benefits for the firms themselves. One possible benefit comes from firms lowering their cost of funds by internationalizing their cost of capital.

INTERNATIONALIZING THE COST OF CAPITAL

Another area supporting equity market development is the internationalization of the cost of capital. Internationalizing the cost of capital leads to potential for lowering costs of funds for firms, creating greater investment opportunities for investors, and obtaining increased investable funds.

"Cost of capital" can be looked at from two different perspectives. The first is the expected cost of funds to finance the activities of the company. The second is one of several discount rates to be applied to future cash flows used when evaluating potential projects. Cost of capital in this section refers to the first perspective, the expected cost of funds, rather than to a rate of discount for projects. The traditional definition of cost of capital in an efficient market is

$$K(a) = K(e) \ [E / V] + K(i) \ [1 - t] \ [D / V]$$

where the variables are the companies' weighted average cost of capital, $K(a)$; expected cost of equity capital, $K(e)$; expected cost of debt before taxes, $K(i)$; marginal tax rate, t; market value of the equity capital, E; market value of the debt capital, D; and total market value of the equity and debt, V.[24]

The expected cost of equity and debt is determined by the return required for investors to hold such securities. The rate of return required by investors is based on investor preferences with respect to risk and return in light of the current market conditions. Investors develop and express their preferences for risk by their decisions to buy, hold, or sell securities. These preferences depend on three factors: market efficiency (discussed earlier), liquidity, and segmentation.

Market Liquidity

A liquidity premium is said to exist in financial markets when a large block of financial securities is sold below the present value of the risk adjusted discounted future cash flows.

Three competing hypotheses on this phenomenon have arisen. The liquidity premium, or price pressure hypothesis, states that a premium would exist only for a transaction period and that the value of the security should recover to the normal price after the transaction is over. The dip in the price is the liquidity premium. The information effect hypothesis postulates that the dip in price is due to the effect of the new information the trade brings to the market. This hypothesis also states that, after the transaction takes place, no rebound in the price is seen. Finally, the substitution hypothesis states, if financial securities are perfect substitutes, no effect in the price should take place if no new information is received.[25]

Studies of testing for liquidity in the U.S. market have been done by many researchers, including Scholes, Kraus and Stoll, and Carey.[26] However, in thin markets the methodologies described are difficult to use.[27] In an important paper for developing countries, Massmann discusses the difficulty in the measurement of the developing country equity markets and could not reject a liquidity premium in the Chilean Stock Market.[28]

Liquidity, in the trading volume sense, refers to the ability to find either a buyer or seller for a specific asset. If there is no efficient securities market in which to buy and sell an asset, the market value of the firm's debt and equity is reduced, brought about by simple supply and demand considerations, while the expected cost of debt and equity is increased (due to the liquidity premium), raising the cost of capital. As national markets are developed, and as national and international markets are integrated, liquidity increases, the liquidity premium decreases, and cost of capital decreases. Thus, companies in countries with liquid capital markets may have a competitive advantage over companies in countries without liquid markets. However, the effect of October 19, 1987, indicated that there are times when even the developed capital markets are not as liquid as investors would like.

Market Segmentation

A capital market is considered segmented if the required rate of return on securities in that market differs from the required rate of return on comparable securities in other national or in international capital markets. Theoretically, if all markets were fully integrated, all assets having the same risk should enjoy the same rate of return in all markets, except for differences in tax brackets.

Finance theorists have questioned whether national capital markets are segmented or integrated with other countries' capital markets. Statistical tests of this question show that there is an element of both international and purely national factors in security prices, causing researchers to concede that capital markets can be both partly integrated and partly segmented.[29]

In analyzing the effect of segmentation on a firm's cost of capital, Stapleton and Subrahmanyam concluded:

> In most cases, the effect of segmented capital markets is to depress security prices and also to produce an incentive for corporations to increase the diversification opportunities available to investors. Three corporate financial policies that effectively reduce the effects of segmented markets are: (a) foreign portfolio/direct investment by firms, (b) mergers with foreign firms, and (c) dual listing of the securities of the firm on foreign capital markets.[30]

This has relevance for developing countries in that a domestic firm's cost of capital can be lowered by eliminating segmentation in the economy. One of the major ways to eliminate segmentation is establishing a domestic securities market.

One of the major papers dealing with the integration issue was written by Subrahmanyam.[31] He showed, using the quadratic, exponential, and logarithmic utility functions, that international capital market integration is pareto-optimal, that the welfare of individuals in the economies considered never declines and will generally improve as capital markets become more integrated.

The review of theory thus far has shown many important benefits attributable to securities markets and equity markets. However, most of the theory and research has been concentrated in the industrialized countries of North America and Europe. This next section will discuss the applied literature regarding securities markets in developing countries.

APPLIED LITERATURE ON SECURITIES MARKETS IN DEVELOPING COUNTRIES

Securities markets in developing countries have received little attention to date. This area has similar beginnings and is often intermixed with the financial development and economic growth literature discussed earlier. Securities markets are considered part of the later stages in the financial development of a country.

Some of the first to discuss securities markets in developing countries were Wai and Patrick.[32] They surveyed existing capital markets and determined that, except for Brazil, their developmental effect was small. They stated:

> Capital markets can play a positive role in development, but it will be initially modest and only gradually increasing. . . . We also support a positive and comprehensive but gradualist approach to capital market development by the government authorities, as vigorous capital market can exist only in a supportive social, political and legal as well as economic environment.[33]

However, they also considered that rapid economic development could occur without the presence of capital markets.

P. J. Drake, looking at the expansion of the Asian securities markets and building on the work of Wai and Patrick, stated that their comprehensive but gradualist approach should be advanced with more vigor and conviction. "The inherent obstacles to securities market development seem to have been overplayed, and the prospects for beneficial community response to positive policies correspondingly understated, in the limited literature."[34] Drake further emphasized that in the right circumstances, it may be justifiable to go a stage further and introduce measures to promote securities markets. He suggested that the empirical work done so far gave some grounds for thinking that the development of securities markets may be more feasible and beneficial than has generally been believed. However, he also cautioned that securities markets should bear promotion only as part of a consistent package of economic policy.

One of the first to put securities market development in terms of the goals and objectives of the developing countries, rather than in terms of grafting Western institutions into entirely different social and economic systems, was Dickie.[35] Dickie noted that motives for developing capital markets in developing countries have been different from those in industrialized countries. Instead of purely a response to private needs for capital, securities markets have been developed to pursue government political and economic goals, such as financial deepening,[36] diversification of company ownership,[37] and transferring foreign ownership to domestic residents.[38] Dickie saw problems in securities markets not as insurmountable barriers but as obstacles to overcome.

One of the authors analyzing the developing countries in Africa took an extremely negative view of actively promoting securities markets in developing countries. Calamanti contended that there was no plausible evidence to suggest that securities markets stimulate economic growth. He suggested that securities markets may

> seriously jeopardize the growth and stability of a country's financial structure, may introduce factors which tend to aggravate, if not originate economic fluctuation, and may adversely affect the allocation of savings, reallocation of existing real wealth, redistribution of income and the conduct of monetary policy.[39]

In a later paper, Drake expressed a rebuttal to this extreme view by stating

> Although this is indeed possible; but in the absence of concrete evidence that LDCs securities markets have generally had such a deleterious effects, this view is no more persuasive that the opposite one that securities market are, on balance, likely to be beneficial to economic development.[40]

The question is still open to debate. However, most of the support for each view has been based on each author's experiences, with very little empirical research to support either view. Because of the complexities of securities markets and the interrelationships among government policy, market forces, and investor behavior, current theoretical and empirical research has yet to produce a conclusive answer to this question.

A major difference between the camps of those for or against supporting securities market development seems to be the view of the inherent problems associated with development. Those supporting securities market development see the inherent problems as obstacles that can be overcome with proper policy, regulation, and foresight. Those against the active promotion of securities markets consider opposition to securities markets as the best way to overcome the obstacles. It seems ironic that many of the past problems ascribed to securities markets have been due not to inherent problems of securities market development but to causes related to improper regulation or establishment of the securities market in question, such as the crash of the Kuwait unofficial and unregulated stock exchange, the Sook Al-manakh. It is also ironic that the outlook of individual writers toward securities markets stems from the countries being analyzed. Those looking at the successful developments in Asia see much more room for optimism than those looking at the situation in Africa (although not all authors looking at the African countries' securities markets are pessimistic).

It is generally agreed that the nature and content of the net benefits that a securities market may confer within a country should be judged by the market's effects on the savings ratio, capital inflow and outflow, the mobility of investable funds, resource allocation, income and wealth distribution, and the scope for monetary policy. Major writers about securities markets in developing countries are also united in refusing to accept a priori any general policy of subsidized securities markets.[41]

Although the academic literature toward securities markets is still somewhat open to question, in a more practical sense, the question has been answered. Multilateral and regional institutions, such as the International Finance Corporation of the World Bank group and the Asian Development Bank, have made major contributions to the literature of securities markets in developing countries.[42] They provide technical assistance on legal issues, regulatory and fiscal policies, institutional frameworks, and overall development strategies.

One of the major contributions to the knowledge of equity markets in developing countries was the development of the Emerging Markets Database (EMDB) of the International Finance Corporation in 1981. This project, under Antoine van Agtmael, assisted by Peter Wall and Vihang Errunza, documented price, dividend, and capitalization changes for more than 200 companies from ten developing countries (representing 40 percent of market capitalization and the most actively traded stocks) beginning in 1975. This was later increased to 17 countries and more than 400 companies. This was the first time that such a comprehensive database had been compiled on developing countries. From this data, price indices were developed allowing the comparison of actual stock performance from developing countries with industrialized countries. Since then, other publications and electronic information services, including Morgan Stanley Capital International, Solomon Brothers, Reuters, and others have slowly included more developing country markets as part of their global market coverage.

From this base of the EMDB, another major contribution was made by Antoine van Agtmael in 1984 with the publication of *Emerging Securities Markets,* which gave detailed securities information on more than 30 developing countries. This book, and his work at the IFC, brought to the forefront the possible benefits to foreign portfolio investment of investing in developing countries. Additional work by Errunza, Donald Lessard, and others has moved the study of these markets from a position of virtual insignificance to one of mainstream international finance.

If the number of countries looking to develop securities markets versus the number of countries with closed securities markets is any indication, the evidence lies with the beneficial effects of securities markets. From 1971 through June 1988, 73 countries have requested and received capital markets assistance in various forms from the International Finance Corporation's Capital Markets Department. In 50 of those countries, the assistance has been specifically for securities market development.[43]

It is generally accepted that without securities markets, harnessing domestic savings for development would be left to self-finance and institutional credit. Given the evidence of banks' bad and doubtful debts in developing countries, the ability of banks to adequately evaluate long-term and high-risk lending, areas more appropriately filled by bond and equity shares, is strongly in question.[44]

The previous discussion establishes the many benefits in theory from creating an equity market in developing countries. However, there are also costs. The next section discusses, from a more pragmatic point of view, the benefits and costs of equity markets in developing countries.

NOTES

1. J. A. Schumpeter, *The Theory of Economic Development* (Cambridge, Mass.: Harvard University Press, 1954), 95–127.

2. John Maynard Keynes, *The General Theory of Employment, Interest and Money* (New York: Harcourt Brace, 1936).

3. Ronald McKinnon, *Money and Capital in Economic Development* (Washington, D.C.: Brookings Institution, 1973), and Edward S. Shaw, *Deepening.*

4. Yoon Je Cho, "Inefficiencies from Financial Liberalization in the Absence of Well-Functioning Equity Markets," *Journal of Money, Credit and Banking* (May 1986): 1.

5. McKinnon, *Money,* 47.

6. Interest rate constraints should not be confused with usury laws of some religions. Usury laws relate to the absence of interest payments; interest rate constraints limit the amount that can be paid or received on money borrowed or lent.

7. Maxwell J. Fry, "Money and Capital or Financial Deepening in Economic Development," *Journal of Money, Credit and Banking* (November 1978), 467.

8. Cho, "Inefficiencies," 11.

9. Dwaight M. Jaffee and Thomas Russell, "Imperfect Information, Uncertainty and Credit Rationing," *Quarterly Journal of Economics* 90 (November 1976): 651–66; J. E. Stiglitz and Andrew Weiss, "Incentive Effects of Terminations," *American Economic Review* 73 (December 1983): 913–27.

10. Stiglitz and Weiss, "Credit Rationing in Markets with Imperfect Information," *American Economic Review* 71 (June 1981): 393–410.

11. Within the context of portfolio analysis, diversification can be defined as combining securities with less than perfectly positively correlated returns. See Jack C. Francis and Stephen H. Archer, *Portfolio Analysis* (Englewood Cliffs, NJ: Prentice-Hall, 1979), 24.

12. The following constraint is placed on all portfolios:

$$\sum_{i=1}^{n} x_i = 1$$

This states that the n fractions of portfolio invested in n different assets add up to 1.

13. For a list of the correlation coefficients for 17 developing countries for the period of 1976–1980, see Antoine van Agtmael, *Emerging Securities Markets* (London: Euromoney Publications, 1984), 38.

14. The advantages of international diversification have long been identified in the literature. For examples see Bruno H. Solnik, "Why Not Diversify Internationally Rather Than Domestically?" *Financial Analyst Journal* (July–August 1974): 48–54; Gary F. Bergstrom, "A New Route to Higher Returns and Lower Risks," *Journal of Portfolio Management* (Autumn 1975): 30–38; Donald Lessard, "World, Country and Industry Relationships in Equity Returns: Implications for Risk Reduction through International Diversifications," *Financial Analysts Journal* (January–February 1976): 2–8; Vihang R. Errunza, "Emerging Markets: A New Opportunity for Improving Global Portfolio Performance," *Financial Analysts Journal* (September–October 1983): 51–58; and Roger G. Ibbotson, Richard C. Carr, and Anthony W. Robinson, "International Equity and Bond Returns," *Financial Analysts Journal* (July–August 1982): 61–83.

15. For a discussion of the current situation, see Eugene F. Fama, "Efficient Capital Markets: A Review of Theory and Empirical Work," *Journal of Finance* 33 (June 1978): 902–17. In addition to market efficiency other than "price," operational, allocational, and structural efficiency are also important.

16. U. Tun Wai and Hugh T. Patrick, "Stock and Bond Issues and Capital Markets in Less Developed Countries," *IMF Staff Papers* 20 (July 1973) 301; Robert B. Dickie, "Development of Third World Securities Markets: An Analysis of General Principles and a Case Study of the Indonesian Market," *Law and Policy in International Business* 13 (1981) 178, 194–196; Jonathan Hakim, ed. *Securities Markets* (Washington, D.C.: IFC, 1985) 13.

17.   Gabriel Hawawini, *European Equity Markets: Price Behavior and Efficiency*, Monograph 4/5 (New York: Salomm Brothers Center for the Study of Financial Institutions, 1984).

18.   Alex Anckonie III and Chang-hyun Chi, "Internationalization of the Korean Stock Market," unpublished manuscript, George Washington University, June 1986.

19.   Devinder Gandhi, Anthony Saunders, and Richard Woodward, "Thin Capital Markets: A Case Study of the Kuwaiti Stock Market," *Applied Economics* 12 (1980): 341–49.

20.   Raul Solis and Alberto Usobiaga, "Returns, Efficiency and Diversification in the Mexican Stock Market," unpublished manuscript, October 1980.

21.   Martin Laurence, "Some Efficiency Characteristics of the Kuala Lumpur and Singapore Stock Markets," paper presented to the Financial Management Association, October 22–24, 1984, Cincinnati, Ohio.

22.   Vihang R. Errunza and Etienne Losq, "The Behavior of Stock Prices on LDC Markets," *Journal of Banking and Finance* 9 (1985): 561–75.

23.   Bryan L. Sudweeks, "Equity Market Development in Developing Countries: General Principles, Case Studies, Portfolio Implications, and Relevance for the People's Republic of China," Ph.D. dissertation, George Washington University, 1987.

24.   Arthur I. Stonehill and Kare B. Dullum, *Internationalizing the Cost of Capital: The Novo Experience and National Policy Implications* (New York: John Wiley & Sons, 1982).

25.   For a more in-depth discussion of the liquidity premium in DCs, see Juan Ricardo Massmann, "Liquidity Premium in the Chilean Stock Market Exchange," paper presented to the Business Association of Latin American Studies, Washington, D.C., 1985.

26.   Myron Scholes, "The Market for Securities: Substitution versus Price Pressure and the Effects of Information on Share Prices," *Journal of Business* 45 (1972): 179–211; Alan Kraus and Hans R. Stoll, "Price Impacts of Block Trading on the New York Stock Exchange," *Journal of Finance* 27 (1972): 569–88; Kenneth Carey, "Nonrandom Price Changes in Association with Trading in Large Block: Evidence of Market Efficiency in Behavior of Investor Returns," *Journal of Business* 50 (1977): 407–14.

27.   Thinness can be defined as the lack of price resilience in successive trades or as the excess volatility of a securities price beyond that due to price adjustment of new information.

28.   Massmann, "Liquidity Premium," 91–93.

29.   Donald Lessard, "World, National and Industry Factors in Equity Returns," *Journal of Finance* 29 (May 1974): 379–91; Bruno Solnik, "The International Pricing of Risk: An Empirical Investigation of the World Capital Market Structure," *Journal of Finance* 29 (1974): 365–78; and Vihang Errunza, "Efficiency and the Program to Develop Capital Markets: The Brazilian Experience," *Journal of Banking and Finance* 3 (1979): 355–82.

30.   R. C. Stapleton and M. G. Subrahmanyam, "Market Imperfections, Capital Market Equilibrium and Corporate Finance," *Journal of Finance* 32 (May 1977): 317.

31.   Marti G. Subrahmanyam, "On the Optimality of International Capital Market Integration," *Journal of Financial Economics* 2 (March 1975): 3.

32.   U. Tun Wai and Hugh Patrick, "Stock and Bond Issues and Capital Markets in Less Developed Countries," *IMF Staff Papers* 20 (July 1973): 253–317.

33.   Wai and Patrick, "Stock and Bond Issues," 301.

34.   P. J. Drake, "Securities Markets in Less-Developed Countries," *Journal of Development Studies* 13 (January 1977): 73–74.

35.   Robert B. Dickie, "Development of Third World Securities Markets: An Analysis of General Principles and a Case Study of the Indonesian Market," *Law and Policy in International Business,* 13 (1981): 177–222.

36.   See generally R. Goldsmith, *Financial Structure,* 1969; and E. Shaw, *Financial Deepening,* 1973.

37.   Thailand is an excellent example. See Uthaisri and Vachratith, "New Life for Corporations," *Asian Finance* (September 15, 1979), 80.

38.   The Indian and Philippine markets are excellent examples.

39.   Andrea Calamanti, *The Securities Market and Underdevelopment: The Stock Exchange in the Ivory Coast, Morocco and Tunisia* (Milan: Finafrica & Guiffre, 1983).

40.   P. J. Drake, "Some Reflections on Problems Affecting Securities Markets in Less Developed Countries," *Savings and Development* 9 (1985): 6.

41.   Major publications and articles covering the general principles of securities markets in developing countries include Antoine van Agtmael, *Emerging,* 1984; Calamanti, *Underdevelopment,* 1983; Dickie, "Development of Third World Securities Markets," 1981; Drake, "Securities Markets," 1977; Wai and Patrick, "Stock and Bond Issues," 1973; and Sudweeks, "Equity Market Development in Developing Countries," 1987. The most comprehensive descriptive discussion of the current situation in developing countries is the seminal work by van Agtmael.

42.   For a list of articles written by the Capital Markets group of the IFC, see the articles by David Gill and Antoine van Agtmael in the bibliography. To expand the work done by these important institutions, the author recommends that this information be made more available to the general public. Studies, such as the million-dollar research project on capital markets in Asia done by the Asian Development Bank (see "Hands-on Policy Hurts: Study Finds Intervention Stunts Capital Markets," *The Far Eastern Economic Review* [January 30, 1986], 46) are very important. They are still unavailable to the general research community although the summary proceedings, *Capital Market Development in the Asia-Pacific Region* (Philippines: Asian Development Bank, 1986), are an excellent reference.

43.   Interview with Peter Wall, research analyst with the Capital Markets Department, International Finance Corporation, November 19, 1988.

44.   P. J. Drake, "Some Reflections on Problems Affecting Securities Markets in Less Developed Countries," *Savings and Development* 9 (1985): 5–15.

3

Benefits and Costs of
Equity Markets in DCs

From the theoretical literature and discussions with experts in equity market development, it is apparent that there are general benefits and costs of equity markets. However, the development of an equity market must be viewed in light of the goals and objectives of a total financial system, rather than as an isolated component. Equity markets are an important part of a country's financial system but not the only part. And although it may be necessary to emphasize equity markets during a particular period of financial system development, the development of an equity market in a country should always be viewed as part of a balanced financial system and as a means toward other more fundamental economic and social policy objectives. If those ultimate objectives are not kept in mind, the benefits and costs are not viewed in their broader perspective.

In many developed and developing countries, government policies have not favored equity markets. Policies seem to favor government intervention versus private initiative, planned allocation versus market allocation, foreign borrowing versus equity base expansion, and debt versus equity as a means of financing growth.

Many governments also support policies that indirectly affect equity markets. These included controls on interest rates at below market levels, which discourage domestic savings; inflation, which discourages long-term financial investment; erratic monetary policies, which favor real estate and other investments; erratic fiscal policies, which favor interest on bank deposits over stock dividends or capital gains; promotion of national insurance companies with requirements to invest in low-yielding government bonds, which discourages the development of pension funds and insurance companies; and establishing public enterprises and price controls for private firms, which discourages the development of the private sector. Indeed, in many countries, distortions and efficiency are overlooked, domestic savings mobilization is not a top priority, and financial discipline takes a back seat to nominal economic growth.

Although developing country officials may possibly understand the macro and micro benefits associated with the development of equity markets in developing countries, many have not proceeded in this area. This is partially because perceived costs, in terms of the institutional, regulatory, and legal environments, have overshadowed the benefits of equity markets. In most DCs this is not the case. This chapter sets out major benefits and costs of equity markets in DCs to allow a more informed position.

BENEFITS OF EQUITY MARKETS

From theory we can see that equity markets can be an important tool for economic development, investment mobilization, and lowering firms' cost of capital. Equity markets have other benefits. Although this research looks only at equity markets, most of what is discussed is equally relevant to securities markets as a whole.

Macro Benefits

Many feel that the only reason for equity markets in economic development is to raise capital. This is a normal but very myopic view of the importance of equity markets. Equity markets perform many other important functions, in addition to raising capital.[1] In the macro area of development these include increased efficiency of the financial system, fund term matching, mobilization of savings, effective allocation of investment, control of the money supply, indigenization of investment, and privatization of productive activities. Moreover, in an important paper, Subrahmanyam has shown that the benefits of opening a country's capital markets are pareto-optimal. The welfare of individuals in the economy considered never declines and will generally improve.[2]

Increased Efficiency of the Financial System

The existence of a well-regulated equity market can increase efficiency of the financial system through competition among different classes of financial instruments, can raise the nominal rates of savings to savers, and can lower the rates to borrowers. The existence of an active market for equities and other securities creates alternatives for savers and borrowers. As alternatives increase, investors can compare yields, and companies can compare differing costs of finance. As institutions compete for the same pool of investable funds, rates become more competitive, higher for investors and lower for borrowers.

In countries with small financial sectors, there is little competition for funds. Monopolistic policies are easily instituted with below-market interest rates and planned allocation. Financial institutions have little incentive to offer lower deposit rates as there are limited legal alternatives to bank deposits.

Where financial ownership of corporations is highly concentrated, oligopolistic tendencies exist, especially when interest rates are limited or controlled. In countries where there is an interlocking of banks and industrial companies, privileged access to credit is granted, often at the expense of other higher return projects. As the base of ownership broadens, these ties theoretically are weakened, with greater separation between these industries.

Equity markets contribute to financial system solvency. The absence of viable equity markets tends to push up debt/equity ratios of corporations, weakening their financial structure. This endangers not only their long term viability but also the solvency of their lenders from the banking system. Where firms use both debt and equity as a means of raising funds, the solvency of the financial system increases.

Because of the lack of financial institutions and instruments, savers are limited in their choices of financial instruments. Where equity markets are developed, savers have greater choice of instruments with differing risk and return characteristics, allowing a greater ability to construct their desired portfolio.

Fund Term Matching

Equity markets also help in fund term matching. Whereas governments and corporations want long-term funds, investors want liquidity, so secondary markets are established. This helps to ensure long-term funds for government (to finance development) and private projects and to ensure liquidity for the investors. This also broadens the investor base of those holding long-term instruments, making the financial system sounder.

Mobilization of Savings

Equity markets aid in mobilizing savings. Investors are quick to respond to changes in the real interest rate, as stated by those of the repressionist school of financial development. When controls cause negative real rates, deposits drop and investors find other ways to invest their money. This could be a transfer into other assets or the common flight of capital to other countries with higher returns. There is indeed a positive association between the degree of development of the financial sector, in particular freer interest rates, and general economic performance in developing countries.[3]

To the extent that equity is a viable and relatively secure form of investment with an attractive long-term return, it serves two functions. It provides an incentive to save and invest rather than to consume, buy land and real estate (thereby fueling speculation in this sector), or seek more profitable investment alternative abroad. It competes with bank deposits, which may be subject to interest rate controls. Financial savings are promoted over nonfinancial savings, and the domestic savings rate overall may increase. Moreover, it exerts pressure to keep the controlled interest rates closer to market rates, which are more likely to reflect current supply and demand conditions.

Effective Allocation of Investment

Effective equity markets force corporations and governments to compete on an equal basis for funds, making investment more efficient. Moreover, poor decisions in the marketplace may have large effects on the price at which the market values a firm. Close relationships between banks and industrial groups can hide poor performance of various member companies by shifting funds between companies. Independent private firms, however, do not have this luxury. Few governments and planned economies can allocate investment as well and as consistently as the decentralized market mechanisms.

An important caveat is that although equity markets are important to this aspect, they cannot raise all development funds. They are, however, an important part of the financial sector and can serve as a safety valve to ensure that distortions caused by governments do not become excessive.

Indigenization of Investment

One of the concerns of developing country governments, especially those dependent on foreign capital and other aid, has been how to free the business sector from foreign control without seriously endangering economic growth. The ability of domestic individuals to purchase shares of the foreign firm, to turn private domestic savings into equity investments, can yield many benefits including continuity in growth, possible greater profit retention in the country, and a greater degree of control by domestic investors.

Privatization of Productive Activities

Another major problem in many countries has been the growth and size of the public sector. With equity markets, the orderly transfer of shares from the government to private investors is possible without disruption and other negative effects. For countries with large public sectors, the ability to transfer activities to the private sector not only increases government revenues but also removes from government concerns many activities that are better performed by the private sector and that may have been a drain on government revenues.

Additional Funding (IDRs and ADRs)

The growth of a domestic equity market may offer additional sources of funds for many companies. Companies that have sufficient market presence internationally may encourage or be encouraged by foreign banks to establish foreign depository receipts to be sold in foreign markets. Through this means the stocks never leave the country, yet additional funding is obtained, name recognition is improved, and the investor base is broadened.[4]

Debt Equity Swaps

With the development of an equity market, the possibility exists for the gradual elimination of portions of a country's debt through activities such as debt equity swaps. In this process, existing bank loans are swapped for new or existing equity in public or private firms, effectively reducing debt service costs, increasing the investor base, and increasing the depth of the local equity market.

Micro Benefits

Most of what we have previously discussed has been in the macro area of development. However, several micro issues should be mentioned: private-sector solvency, broadening of the ownership base, access for new companies, and improved accounting standards.

Private-Sector Solvency

In countries where there is no equity market, firms often use short-term credit and bank overdrafts to meet their working capital needs, resulting in a mismatch of maturities between assets and liabilities. Moreover, in these situations, debt-to-equity ratios rise, resulting in greater risks for the company and its present investors. Should a firm be capitalized enough to be able to turn to the Eurocredit market, the floating rate nature of the borrowed funds may still create problems for many firms.

Broadening of the Ownership Base

We have already discussed the problems of relationships between banks and some industries. If there is no viable equity market, companies must turn to banks in order to meet their short- and long-term capital requirements. Often, access to funds is ensured by seeking control of a few banks. But banks may also branch out by requiring equity stakes as a condition for financing. As their equity stakes increase, these financial-industrial groups can grow into quasi-money and capital markets, effectively allocating funds on the basis of the firms they control rather than on the investment opportunities themselves. The problems of inefficiency and overinvestment are easily disguised, and, when serious problems arise, they can cause major negative repercussions for both the industrial companies and the banks.

Access for New Companies

Functioning equity markets in many countries play an important role in allocating risk capital. Investors with greater inclinations to risk, such as venture capital firms or their equivalent, are much more willing to invest if opportunities for divestment or going public through stock offerings exist.

Improved Accounting/Tax Standards

As security markets grow, investors request more and better information to compare performance among firms and countries. It becomes in the firms' best interest to provide that information to ensure adequate comparisons between competing firms and countries. Improved accounting standards also benefit in better decision making for firms and possible better tax information for governments.

Improved Access to Foreign Equity

With the growth of a domestic equity market, foreign firms may seek to list on the domestic exchange. With the addition of foreign firms, investors' alternatives are increased, including possible opportunities for higher returns. Profits from executing transactions remain with domestic firms if done through local brokers.

COSTS OF EQUITY MARKETS

Equity markets are not without cost. In addition to the costs that can occur through uncertain political, economic, financial, legal, and tax environments, certain problems inherent in the system cannot be avoided. These include the inevitability of market cycles, interest rate fluctuations, intermediation costs, the need for additional regulation, loss of some control over the financial system, possibilities of speculation and dishonest activities, and inefficient allocation from a national perspective.

Inherent Problems

The Inevitability of Market Cycles

Markets react quickly to domestic and international events, often with the level and causal relationship unclear. Moreover, market cycles have a large impact on the raising of capital. During the early stages of development, markets are more susceptible to market cycles because of low numbers of stocks, easier possibility of manipulation, and unsophisticated and inexperienced investors, underwriters, and brokers.

Activities in the secondary markets may also undermine investors' confidence in the primary market. Secondary market activities can have a large effect on the ability of companies to raise funds.

Investor Confidence and Financial System Strength

In developing equity markets, investor confidence is often low because of the newness of the system. Knowledge of the financial system is often misunderstood and is sometimes at odds with traditional financing techniques.

Moreover, the strength of the financial system is limited because of limited experience of most investors (where markets are developing) with investment as a whole and with domestic investment in particular.

The size of the markets often causes developing country markets to suffer from dangers of monopolistic controls and instability of prices and rates.

Interest/Exchange Rate Fluctuations

One of the constants of today's markets is the inevitability of interest rate fluctuations. Although a problem for financial planning, it offers governments a tool for monetary policy.

One of the major government policies that affect equity markets is the setting of interest rates. Although it seems that firms will obtain credit also at low rates, if the government establishes artificially low interest rates for borrowers, this rarely happens. Because financial institutions will pay lower rates on deposits if loan rates are low, interest rate repression leads to capital outflows and foreign exchange shortages that negatively impact the overall economic climate.

"Although positive real interest rates are likely to be beneficial in the long run, the experience of countries such as Brazil, Argentina, Chile and others demonstrates that, after periods of substantially negative real rates, high positive real rates can be expected during the adjustments period following liberalization."[5] Even if temporary, this problem may be quite severe.

Exchange rate policies also are important, especially as the developing countries are becoming more integrated into the world economy. Volatile exchange rates affect the amount of foreign funds coming or leaving a country's capital markets.

Intermediation Costs

The intermediation costs of the equity exchange and equity market institutions may be large. In addition to an actual equity exchange and public and private regulatory agencies, equity markets require large numbers of support personnel to handle the underwriting, brokerage, investment analysis, and investment activities. If these activities are not already part of the countries' current financial structure, preparing the financial structure necessary for the markets could be both costly and time consuming.

However, virtually all costs of equity markets can be funded by those who benefit. The stock exchange obtains fees from the companies listed, companies pay the costs of providing financial information, underwriters receive fees from the issuers, brokers receive fees from both the issuers and investors, investment analysts receive fees from the investors, and expenses for the equity agencies may be partially offset by registration fees.

Need for Additional Regulation

Countries with developing equity markets require regulation of a separate subsector of the financial system. Although part of the costs may be offset by registration fees, it is often hard to satisfy the population that the benefits exceed the costs of a domestic equity market.

Loss of Some Control of the Financial System

In many countries, the financial system is composed only of banks or other similar institutions. Government policy is enforced through direct control of the granting or withholding of credit to public and private institutions. With the establishment of equity markets, there is less direct control over the countries' financial system (i.e., if there is tight monetary policy, the companies have the option to sell equity). Therefore, instead of direct control, countries must use indirect methods to achieve their monetary objectives.

At the individual level, other types of loss of control are discernible. It is often in the financial and political interests of those granting licenses not to establish equity markets in order to perpetuate their power and the power of their friends. Equity markets cause the loss of some of this control.

Possibilities for Speculation and Dishonest Activity

Stock markets may encourage speculation both by individuals and institutions that, followed by collapse, can lead to the ruin of both. Wall Street in the late 1920s, Hong Kong in 1973, and the unofficial Sook Al-manakh in Kuwait in 1982 are three striking examples. Stock markets also can provide an arena for dishonest activity, such as conflict of interest, market rigging, insider trading, and issuing false or misleading prospectuses — problems still encountered by developed industrial markets. Careful regulation can reduce these problems.

Inefficient Allocation of Investment from a National Perspective

Although stock markets may allocate funds to the activities that are expected to show the greatest financial profit, from a national viewpoint these may not be the profitable, given the often distorted financial markets in many developing countries. However, governments retain authority to prohibit private-sector investments it considers not in the national interest.

In addition, the market mechanism will not allocate resources to socially needed programs that yield a social benefit rather than a monetary profit. Government regulation is necessary in order to provide for these social programs.

External Sources of Concern

Loss of Local Ownership

Because the shares of many companies can be bought on the stock exchange, there is a possibility that a foreign investor or corporation can purchase the necessary share and obtain controlling ownership of the firm. In many countries where companies listed on the exchange are very small, this is a major concern. Legal methods can be established to alleviate this concern, which will be discussed later.

Destabilizing Money Flows

In countries where foreign investors are allowed free access to local markets, there is the possibility of destabilizing money flows in and out of the country, with the attendant impact on money supply and inflation. Governments are reluctant to open their markets because of their inability to control or plan for foreign inflows of funds.

Challenge to Established Ideas

A final cost (or benefit, depending on the point of view) of equity markets, sometimes more important than all others, is the challenge to established ideas. The development of equity markets challenges certain key ideas that may have been critical to the historical development of a country. These include the ideas that officials can allocate resources and interest rates better than the marketplace; that problems can be solved by making the government enterprises run better (i.e., more bureaucracy); that even if a market is established, a future government will change the rules, so why change now? and, finally, that foreign capital is foreign domination.

Because an equity market challenges these established ideas and beliefs, some individuals and governments have difficulty accepting it. First, the market mechanism can allocate resources better than central planners can. Experience in developing countries has shown this to be the case. Many governments have also attempted through legislative fiat, to limit the amount of interest charged on loans and paid on savings in an attempt to ensure additional loanable funds and profitability for banks. But firms and investors are quick to realize the real rate of interest. Where subsidized credit exists, there is no incentive for firms to go to the equity markets, limiting the depth of those markets. Where interest rates are held at below market rates and equity markets do not exist, investors are quick to shift from deposits to consumption, gold, real estate, or capital flight. This is not to say that there are not problems with an unrestrained market mechanism; however, there are means to correct those problems.

Second, more bureaucracy will not solve all the problems. In fact, it is usually contrary to the best interests of the company and country. Reducing bureaucracy is very difficult. It builds on itself, and as the original need for bureaucracy is eliminated, the bureaucracy will continue. It is often in the best interests of those in power to continue with established lines of authority (power) in order to remain in power. Anything that might reduce that authority (i.e., a reduction in bureaucracy) is contrary to the interests of those in authority.

Third, even though the possibility of future change exists, governments should still act. The possibility of future change should not restrict current action that is in the long-term interest of the country or investors.

And fourth, foreign investment is not foreign domination. There are benefits, as discussed earlier, to inflows of foreign capital. And means can be established whereby the major objections to foreign capital can be reduced. Foreign capital can be beneficial to the long-term growth in developing countries.

The establishment of an equity market in DCs may exact a heavy price from certain ideas important to the development of that country. However, the growth of stock exchanges in socialist and communist countries, such as the development of exchanges in the People's Republic of China and Hungary, give reason to believe that these are not insurmountable barriers.

NOTES

1. A more extensive discussion of the benefits and costs of equity markets can be found in Antoine van Agtmael, *Emerging Securities Markets*.

2. Marti G. Subrahmanyam, "On the Optimality of International Capital Market Integration," *Journal of Financial Economics* 2 (March 1975): 3.

3. Sebastian Edwards and Mohsin S. Khan, "Interest Rates in Developing Countries," *Finance and Development* (June 1985), 28.

4. For a better understanding of foreign depository receipts (ADRs in the United States) see Gerald Warfield, *How to Buy Foreign Stocks and Bonds* (New York: Harper & Row, 1985), 24–31.

5. van Agtmael, *Emerging Securities,* 10.

4

General Conditions for Equity Market Development

Evaluation of development activities in various developing countries and the analysis of current research reveals that the environment of a developing country plays an important part in the success or failure of an equity market development program. To the extent that the environment is conducive, the market develops much quicker than in countries where the environment is hostile. Rather than a single environment, the structure of developing countries is multifaceted, relating to the economic, political, legal, institutional, and regulatory environments and to the interest/exchange rate, taxation, institutional investors, and foreign participation policies. Each concept need not be fully implemented for a successful development program; however, to the extent that these conditions are supportive, the greater the probability that the market will grow and develop.

ENVIRONMENTS

Economic Environment

Economic growth is an important factor in the development of an equity market in a country. Economies dominated by government enterprises or with scarce entrepreneurial experience may find it difficult to develop the market. However, even socialist countries can have a strong equity market should they decide to pursue a course consistent with some degree of a market economy.

Education is an important area. Without an educated population, especially in reference to the use of financial assets versus real assets, the

49

market may not develop. Moreover, an educated population may increase the number of available professionals (businessmen, accountants, financial analysts, and regulatory analysts), which are necessary to the development of the institutional and regulatory environment.

The presence of an increasing level of disposable household savings is important to the development of the market. Investors will invest only after they have met their basic needs.

Sustainable positive rates of economic growth lead to new markets, greater opportunities for firms to grow (and make a profit), strong inducements for firms to obtain finance through raising equity to expand operations, and greater confidence in the economic system.

Rational monetary policies ensure greater confidence in the stability of the economy. Confidence in financial assets, including equities, improves, and these become vehicles for greater savings mobilization. Policies take into account effects on equity markets, especially the fact that investors are concerned with real returns, not just nominal returns. Policies must ensure an attractive long-term yield for equities in comparison with other domestic and foreign investment alternatives. Frequent devaluations and negative real rates of return force investors to move to other, less risky assets or countries (capital flight).

An economy large enough to support an equity market is also a necessary prerequisite. Without a sufficient supply of equities, trading will be thin, liquidity will be limited, and the market may not be economically justifiable. In cases such as these, regional exchanges may be a viable alternative.

Indigenous entrepreneurs are important contributors to equity market development. There needs to be a continuing supply of new firms coming to the market or existing firms issuing additional shares.

There also must be a separation of ownership/management in some companies for the markets to development. Where firms are closely held and are financed primarily through borrowings, the risk of the firm and cost of capital may increase, and the supply of shares to the market may be lessened.

Finally, inflation should be reasonable. Inflation is one of the market's worst enemies. Should inflation exist, markets still may develop, but accounting practices and financial instruments must be adjusted to handle the uncertainties and problems of companies in the inflationary environment.

Political Environment

Investors are very sensitive to political uncertainty. In countries with border conflicts or domestic turmoil, there is little interest in investing in shares because equity is usually a medium- to long-term form of investment. Political disruption always affects economic activity because companies postpone investments, curtail growth projections, and attempt to move critical activities to more stable countries.

Reasonable political stability is an important element. Equity markets may exist in socialist countries as long as two factors exist: that the generally understood range of possible government actions will not drastically affect the market or the major participants in the market and that there is a less than complete reliance on central planning. Market signals play a critical part in the allocation decision. When these are affected in any way, the efficiency of investment is decreased. The recent beginnings of equity markets in China and Hungary and the equity markets in some of the socialist European countries are a few examples.

Investors are very concerned with the possibilities of nationalization. Investors will not invest if they believe that the company may soon be nationalized or that they may not be paid within a short period of time. Investors are usually the ones who lose from nationalized firms, either from not getting a fair market value for their shares or from having to wait for long periods of time before they are paid for their shares.

The existence of a private sector is important for the development of an equity market. Without a private sector, there may not be an equity market because purely public firms could not be listed. Generally, governments do not sell shares in purely public firms. However, China's recent issuing of minority position shares in which the government holds a majority position is an exception to this general rule.

A sense of confidence about the future is also important. Without confidence in the future, firms would not expand operations, seek new markets, or strive to become more competitive. Equity market development is for firms and countries with confidence in the future.

Legal Environment

Outside investors need to be protected against stock manipulation and improper actions by insiders (major shareholders, directors, and management). In addition, adequate standards of professional conduct by brokers, underwriters, and accountants must be established to avoid excessive speculation caused by market rumors and too easy availability of market loans.

There must also be a favorable environment and legal framework within which business and corporations can operate. This framework must be concerned with the protection of shareholders without seriously affecting the company's ability to finance operations. This legal framework must consider private and public companies equal and thus not give public firms an unfair advantage over private firms.

Institutional Environment

Equity markets cannot function without an effective system of intermediaries including brokers, dealers, and underwriters. In developing countries, these intermediary activities may be performed by the banks as the market is beginning to develop but should become independent as soon as financially viable.

The institutional framework must have an adequate infrastructure for the orderly communication, transfer of information, pricing of issues, marketing of equities, and settlement of securities. Communication facilities must be adequate to relay information between buyers and sellers. Beginnings of an institutional system for transmitting information regarding price, market, and company to the public is necessary for instilling confidence and knowledge about companies and information, especially as domestic individual and institutional investors become more sophisticated. Pricing of issues must be reasonable as companies consider the all-in cost of funds in evaluating funding alternatives. Effective financial institutions for the marketing of equities must be developed also as stocks are sold, not bought. And finally, clearing mechanisms must be established for the quick and efficient settlement of securities.

Important decisions on how to handle off-exchange trading also must be made. International experience has shown that in the initial stages of an equity market, preventing off-exchange trading, although decreasing liquidity somewhat, has led to greater confidence and less speculation in the market. The experience in Kuwait is a case in point. As markets develop and the regulatory machinery is in place, allowing regulated off-exchange trading at a future time may lead to greater liquidity for equities.

Sufficient trained personnel are also a necessary prerequisite. In-house training programs, sending students and professionals abroad to study, bringing in qualified academicians and professionals to train, or sending local professionals to work with international banks and other intermediaries are possible ways of increasing the number of trained personnel.

Within the institutional environment, banks should not have complete control over the financial system and companies; there must be alternatives to bank finance. Limited segmentation of the financial system leads to greater efficiencies, lower costs to issuers, and a more efficient allocation of investment.

Finally, a framework for the creation of an institutional investor market, including the development of insurance companies, mutual funds, and funded pension funds, should be established. Because they are usually the largest investors in equity markets in both developed and developing countries, institutional investors play an important role in the development and maturation process in equity markets.

Regulatory Environment

Markets need some type of regulation to ensure consistency, fairness, and an orderly market. Too often when discussing regulation and equity markets, one impression of the U.S. Securities and Exchange Commission (SEC) comes to mind — the policeman role. However, the SEC was established after the securities industry was an important part of the U.S. financial system.

Regulation in developing equity markets must take a broader view. Major goals must be education and improving investor confidence, encouraging market growth, regulation, and institution building (including developing the necessary regulatory personnel).

The purpose of regulation is to increase investor confidence. Regulation is likely to be unsatisfactory if simply left to the market. The experience in Hong Kong in 1973 is a case in point. Establishing a securities commission was a major factor in restoring investor confidence in the market. The question is the nature of the supervision and the degree of responsibility accorded to securities industry associations. The balance must be drawn between inefficient or inadequate regulation (which may result in rampant speculation, damage to savers, and loss of market confidence) and overregulation (which could stifle initiative and make companies reluctant to go public). The balance can be struck by cooperation among the government, the self-regulatory securities associations, and other established securities associations.

Effective regulation should include brokerage system regulation, minimum disclosure standards, and acceptable accounting and auditing standards.

POLICIES

Interest Rate and Exchange Rate Policy

Interest rate policy has a great effect on the desirability of equity in an individual's portfolio of assets. Controlled interest rates, i.e., rates either below or above market rates, affect equities as individuals seek the highest return for a given level of risk. Should rates on deposits be greater than expected returns on equities, investors will put money in deposit accounts. Likewise, should deposit rates be set at an artificially low ceiling, money will move into other higher yielding alternatives or used for consumption purposes.

Consistent with a market driven economy, it is considered better if interest and exchange rates are not controlled. If rates are controlled, however, a market can still develop, assuming that there is some flexibility in interest rates, especially for securities instruments, and that the rates are monitored closely in the parallel unofficial markets as an indicator of market sentiment. One of the major tools in Korea ensuring that controlled rates were not too divergent was the monitoring of the unofficial interest rates. When the discrepancy between the official and unofficial rates got too wide, official rates were raised. Government officials must remember that rates on competing instruments of equal risk should be equivalent and that investors are concerned about real, not just nominal, returns.

If a government is serious about attracting foreign funds, reasonable monetary exchange rate policies must exist. Moreover, understanding the effect of foreign exchange regulations on international investors to limit negative consequences will do much to develop the market in this area.

Taxation Policy

Investors are concerned with the after-tax real return on investment. Because taxation directly influences this amount, it has a great effect on the development of an equity market. The major concern is that equities be taxed equally with other alternatives. For example, if bank deposit interest is free of taxation, and dividends are subject to a 20 percent withholding tax, then equities are not taxed equally with deposit rates, and banks have an advantage. The rationale behind this action probably developed from a "savings mobilization" objective for bank deposits and a "wealth distribution" objective for dividend income.

Eliminating disincentives to investing in equities is also necessary. The classic example is that of double (even triple) taxation — taxation at the corporate level before distribution and taxation again at the individual level. If returns are taxed by the government of the international investors, there may be triple taxation.

Reasonable corporation taxes aid development. High corporate taxation limits the amount available for dividend distribution, which may affect investors' willingness to invest.

Taxation policy also affects supply of equities. To be effective, tax inducements to go public must offset decreases in possibilities for tax evasion. This can be done through either increasing the tax incentive or increasing scrutiny of closed companies.

Institutional Investors Policy

Institutional investors play an important role in many equity markets, even in developing countries. Guidelines for prudent investments by institutional investors, with proper concern for diversification, are important. However, limiting the possible range of assets for insurance company reserves, mutual funds, or pension schemes to low-yielding government securities (or a high percentage of government securities) has a major dampening effect on market development. In addition, not including equities as allowable assets for institutional investors will definitely affect the development of the market. Private parties and government officials often are not sufficiently aware of the potential importance of institutional investors. Without them, there is great risk of a market dominated by individual speculators.

Foreign Participation Policy

Foreign portfolio investment has played only a minor role in most developing countries, although it does play an important role in countries such as Hong Kong, Singapore, Malaysia, and Mexico. In many other markets, access to domestic markets for foreign portfolio investment is discouraged or is slowly improving.

Foreign portfolio investment is mainly concerned with long-term return and risk diversification, rather than management and control. However, surprisingly few countries have given special incentives to portfolio investment, as opposed to incentives for direct investment.

Foreign portfolio investment is important to a host country because it increases demand for equities, which may lead to new issues by existing companies; creates a demand for better information, which may ultimately benefit local investors; is an additional source of funds for development, in addition to local and borrowed resources; and is often countercyclical to local investors and may help stabilize the market.

For foreign participation to be a viable source of funds, foreign investors need the assurance that they can repatriate their funds. However, many DCs are concerned about the outflows of local currency. Many countries minimize this problem by using closed-end funds, U.S. and international depository receipts, and country funds.

Allowing or requiring some firms, which are usually represented in the home market, to list a portion of their equity may aid domestic investors because of the possibilities of lower correlations with the local market. Allowing domestic firms to list internationally or through U.S. or international depository receipts may be an additional source of funds, in addition to spreading the investor base and aiding in pricing efficiency of the firm. Should stock pricing in one country not conform to the exchange adjusted price in the local market, investors would have the added benefit of arbitrage to adjust the price.

Many countries such as India, Thailand, Korea, Brazil, Malaysia, Greece, and Taiwan have encouraged foreign investments through country funds, bringing additional funds to the market without the worries of traditional international portfolio investment. This has been shown to be a viable intermediary step to internationalization of the markets in many countries. Foreign investors have generally been favorable to these funds, which have often sold at high premiums to net asset value.

Preparing an environment in which equity markets can develop is a major challenge to many developing countries. However, to the extent that these areas discussed are encouraged and developed, there is a greater probability that the equity market will grow. Equity markets can flourish primarily within this type of suitable environment. An overview of the areas discussed in this chapter is shown in Table 4.1.

TABLE 4.1
Conditions for a Successful Equity Market

Economic Environment

The presence of an increasing level of disposable household savings

Sustainable positive rates of economic growth

Rational monetary policies; take into account effects on equity markets

Some development of a middle class

Economy large enough to support a market

Existence of indigenous entrepreneurs

Separation of ownership/management in some companies

Mild inflation; accounting practices and financial instruments adjustable to handle the inflationary environment

Growing view that financial assets are a good investment; view that real assets not only good investments

Political Environment

Reasonable political stability; general understanding of range of possible government actions likely to be selected; general procedural understanding

Limited possibilities of nationalization

Existence of a private sector

Sense of confidence about the future

Less than complete reliance on central planning

Legal Environment

Favorable environment and legal framework within which business and corporations can operate

Private and public enterprises considered equal under the law

Adequate company law for protection of shareholders without seriously affecting the company's ability to finance operations

Adequate securities legislation to protect minority shareholders

Legal system in which disputes resolved within a short period of time

Institutional Environment

Existence of other alternatives to bank finance

Banks do not have complete control over financial system and companies

Effective financial institutions for the marketing of equities

continued

Table 4.1, continued

Existence of brokers, dealers, and underwriters; may be performed by the banks as the market is beginning to develop

Sufficient trained personnel

An adequate supply of fairly priced equities

Limited segmentation of the financial system

Beginnings of an institutional system for making data available to the public; price and market information; company information

An acceptable settlement scheme; decision on how to handle off-exchange trading

Funded pension funds

Beginnings of an institutional investor market, including the development of insurance companies and mutual funds

Adequate communications

Reasonable pricing scheme to buy and sell shares

Regulatory Environment

Exchange self-regulation as major tool

Oversight by government agency; view of government agency as development institution; agency should actively promote the market; goal to provide confidence in system

Sufficient trained regulatory personnel

Effective brokerage system regulation

Minimum disclosure standards

Acceptable accounting and auditing standards

Interest Rate/Exchange Rate Policy

Best if not controlled

If controlled; rates equal on competing instruments of equal risk; concern for real returns

Some flexibility in interest rates, especially for securities instruments

Reasonable monetary exchange rate policies

Understanding of the impact of foreign exchange regulations on international investors

Taxation Policy

Taxation of competing instruments equal

Equities taxed equally with other alternatives

continued

Table 4.1, continued

Elimination of disincentives to market development

If goal is long-term capital, no tax on capital gains

Reasonable corporation taxes because high corporate taxation limits dividend distribution

Adequate taxation policies that limit double taxation for domestic and international investors

Tax inducements to go public to offset decreases in possibilities for tax evasion

Institutional Investors Policy

Guidelines for prudent investments by institutional investors; diversification

Limited numbers of required government securities

Inclusion of equities as allowable assets for institutional investors

Funded pension funds with a fair amount of freedom to invest assets; similar to ERISA legislation

Foreign Participation Policy

Limited amounts of foreign firms (who are in the domestic market) listed on the market may be helpful to pricing structure

Allowing listing of domestic firms in other markets also helpful to pricing structure and raising funds

Encouraging foreign investments through country funds and other means as an alternative source of funds for companies; repatriation of profits must be allowed

5

Measures to Develop the Supply of Shares

Increasing the supply of shares is important, especially during the early stages of the development of an equity market. An increased supply helps create more market liquidity and ensures that measures to stimulate demand will not simply inflate prices of existing equities. Having insufficient stock issues to trade adequately is often a greater constraint on the development of the market than the number of investors. Taiwan is a case in point. Too few stocks deter the public from entering the market at all; later, when trading is active, too many people chasing too few stocks causes the market to rise artificially, with corresponding corrections to come later (i.e., greater volatility).

Investors need a reasonable choice of both government securities and company stock so that they can set up a portfolio as desired. This implies that there must be a supply of companies willing to make their shares available to the public. Van Agtmael suggests that a stock market start with at least 20 companies, each with a float of about 25 percent.[1]

Although they do not directly encourage the flow of savings into equities, supply incentives are important parallel measures in meeting the ultimate objectives of increasing economic efficiency and financial stability. Supply incentives can take several forms. The objective is, by granting to public companies tax or other advantages that are denied to private or closed companies, encouraging companies to go public.

Companies have many reasons to remain closed. Major reasons include fear of loss of control and greater disclosure requirements. Loss of control is a major fear of owners and management, especially in closely held family firms. Such companies should not be required to

61

issue all of their shares to the public. A portion of outstanding shares is sufficient.

Disclosure requirements are another area of concern. Owners of companies worry that disclosure may lead to loss of competitive advantages and to visibility of undervalued or unlisted assets and profits. Governments should avoid placing a listed company at a competitive disadvantage by having excessive disclosure requirements in relation to a nonlisted company. The major goal should be to treat both listed and nonlisted companies equally. If all companies, public and private, were subject to the same rules and regulations, the loss of competitive advantage should be comparable across companies. Because investors' willingness to invest is dependent on the availability and quality of company information, the disclosure standards should improve as the market develops.

The second major reason for firms not wanting to disclose information is that it is to their advantage not to do so. With undervalued assets and understated profits on the books, tax payments to the government are less, increasing the firm owners' personal profits. A major remedy used to control for this problem in many countries is to have a differential corporate tax rate, which is usually 10 percent lower for listed companies than for nonlisted companies. The goal is to make operations more profitable for listed companies than for nonlisted companies, taking into account the amount of assumed profits hidden for tax avoidance by nonlisted companies. A side benefit from efforts to increase the supply of securities is from increased tax collection resulting from more accurate disclosure by companies. Another possible incentive, which may achieve the same objective, would be to have greater disclosure requirements for unlisted versus listed companies.

Supply incentives are used to encourage companies to "open up" to the public. As such, they must address the companies' concerns for not going public. These included lower corporate income taxes, other tax incentives, dividend exemption benefits, exemptions from transfer taxes, exemptions from wealth taxes, and nontax benefits.

TAX INCENTIVES

Lower Corporate Tax Rates

The most commonly used incentive is a lower corporate income tax rate for open companies. Van Agtmael recommends a minimum differential of at least 10 percentage points (assuming a corporate tax rate of 40–50 percent for closed companies) to have an appreciable effect. The effectiveness of this differential may be increased further when the tax authorities pay special attention to companies that are obvious candidates for going public but have not done so. Such an effort may be formally announced or pursued quietly. Either way, word will spread quickly that, from a tax perspective, remaining closed may not be advantageous.

Other Tangible Tax Benefits

Other incentives may aid in increasing the supply of equity. Open companies may receive other benefits, such as exemption of dividends from taxes, eligibility for tax holidays not available to closed companies, special depreciation allowances, and special allowances for bad debts.

Dividend Exemption Benefits

Not only companies themselves but also the existing owners may be offered tax incentives to induce them to go public. Dividends declared by open companies may be declared exempt from dividend tax or may be subject to a lower than usual tax.

Reduced Transfer Benefits

After a company goes public, both major owners and new shareholders may be exempted from a tax (which may exist or be introduced) on the transfer of shares from one shareholder to another. A variant would be an exemption from a portion of the inheritance tax on shareholdings in open companies.

Exemption from Wealth Tax

Many countries have wealth taxes for holdings over a specific amount of shares. Assets held in the form of equity (or bonds) may be exempted from the wealth tax for this type of incentive.

NONTAX BENEFITS

Special nontax benefits may be allowed open firms. In Jordan, new businesses are allowed limited liability status only if they offer a minimum percentage of their equity to the general public (25 percent for financial institutions, 50 percent for industrial and commercial companies). The rationale is that limited liability is a privilege and that controlling shareholders must be prepared to allow the public to buy shares at the same price as the promoter of the company. The extraordinary development of Jordan's equity market is directly attributable to this law.

Open firms also may be given other special nontax benefits, such as priority access to subsidized credits and government contracts. However, this would further complicate existing market distortions and could further limit competition. Such measures may be undesirable on other grounds.

Of the incentives discussed, the most attractive measure has been the lower corporate income tax. It has been proven successful in a number of countries. It removes a disincentive rather than creating an incentive; it does not create any single new distortion from an economic or social point of view; and it is flexible, either adjusted as time goes by or subject to a specific time limit. As a final measure, the law can require companies to issue a portion of their shares to the public. Although not a recommended action, it has been used successfully in Korea to open previously closely held companies.

Measures to develop the supply of shares are important to the development of an equity market. The experience of Brazil and the 157 funds is a good example of what can happen when the supply is not adequately developed to meet demand. Also of importance are measures to develop the demand for equity. Supply and demand must be developed together.

NOTE

1.   Float is defined as the number of shares available to the general public and outside institutional investors for trading, as opposed to being owned by the original founders of the company or other insiders. See van Agtmael, *Emerging Securities*, 22, 45.

6

Measures to Develop the Demand for Shares

Whereas measures to develop the supply of shares are directed at increasing the number of listed companies and the float of shares available to the general public, demand incentives are directed toward those institutions or individuals most likely to become investors. Demand incentives work by removing existing tax disincentives, increasing after-tax yield on equities, or lowering their purchase cost. Some demand incentives are instrument-specific; others are concerned only to promote long-term savings in general. Demand incentives fall under different categories: removal of tax disincentives, indirect purchase incentives, direct purchase incentives, and contractual and collective savings.

REMOVAL OF TAX DISINCENTIVES

The prime example of a tax disincentive is double taxation. It creates a bias in favor of debt because, in most countries, a company can deduct its interest payments in full from its pretax income, yet it cannot deduct its dividend payments. In addition, because individuals are taxed twice on their share of corporate profits and corporations are taxed only once, shares are more attractive to corporations than to individuals.

Other tax disincentives discriminate against equities. In an inflationary environment, capital gains taxes on nominal returns can sharply reduce, or even eliminate, the real return on equities. This causes investors to move to other instruments. The near doubling of the capital-gains tax rate in the United States in 1969–1976 is a good example of what can happen. This doubling of the tax rate is widely blamed for the virtual demise of the market in new issues, which plunged from an annual US$3,500 million to US$247 million in 1977.

Other examples of discrimination against equities are easy to find. Government securities and bank deposits often are exempted from the wealth tax or transfer taxes while equities are taxed at the legal limit.

PURCHASE INCENTIVES

Indirect

Indirect purchase incentives increase the after-tax return to investors. These indirect incentives rely on future uncertain returns on investments rather than on immediate and certain tax benefits to equity buyers.

Examples of indirect purchase incentives include widening the gap between the tax rate applied to retained earnings versus distributed earnings, to give dividends a greater allowance; increasing tax credits for dividends; lowering capital-gains taxes; treating losses more favorably; and lowering overall taxes for corporations.

Experience in the United States has shown that tax changes that affect the investment incomes of shareholders have a greater influence on equity investment than do tax changes that affect corporate profits. However, unless the tax changes are very large, indirect purchase incentives generally do not generate much response.

Direct

Direct incentives reduce the all-in cost of purchasing equities by allowing investors to deduct all or part of the cost from taxes they owe or from their taxable incomes. Direct purchase incentives are normally much more effective than indirect ones, both because they are clear and immediate and because their cash value to taxpayers is normally greater than that of an indirect one, which affects only the rate of return on investments already made. Brazil used this type of incentive effectively when it allowed a credit on taxes for a portion of funds invested in the securities markets.

CONTRACTUAL AND COLLECTIVE SAVINGS

Most governments encourage the growth of contractual and collective savings institutions such as pension funds, insurance companies, or mutual funds. Some of the most common incentives include allowing investors to deduct premium payments or pension contributions from tax; allowing contributions to accumulate tax free; exempting from tax any income received from savings; and deferring any tax liability until savers retire, when their incomes (and tax rates) are lower. The Individual Retirement Account in the United States is an excellent example.

In addition, many countries have portfolio composition requirements stipulating that a certain percentage of collective or contractual savings must be invested in certain types of financial instruments. The inclusion of equities in these requirements is an aid to developing the market. Some countries also offer tax incentives to investors in mutual funds and unit trust, which concentrate on investing in local companies or priority sectors of the economy.

7

Portfolio Implications of Investing in DCs

The previous discussions show that benefits accrue from the development of an equity market in developing countries. However, for equity markets to achieve their full potential there must be a gradual opening of a country's equity markets to the international community. Four major questions are important to equity markets in developing countries. First, is there a large enough pool of international investable funds to make foreign portfolio investment (FPI) a viable source of funds for developing countries? Second, would developing country equities be of interest to international investors? Third, would international equities be of interest to developing country investors? And fourth, what are the implications to investors and governments of opening local and international markets to international investment? This chapter discusses these questions and the possible intermediate steps for DCs considering international investment as an additional source of funds and as an important contributor to the development of an equity market.

FOREIGN PORTFOLIO INVESTMENT

FPI as a Source of Funds

Total global unit trust and mutual fund industry assets are estimated at US$500–600 billion, while the industry is in a relatively early stage of development. In addition, the U.S. pension fund industry has approximately US$700 billion in assets, and many plan sponsors intend to invest 10 percent of these assets in foreign stock markets. To date they have invested US$20 billion in foreign equities. This figure is anticipated to grow to US$45–50 billion over the next ten years. In addition, the Japanese are beginning to invest in offshore equity, and this too may be an additional source of funds. These figures indicate that a large and growing amount of international funds exists. Clearly, FPI may be a viable source of funds for developing countries.

Interest of DC Equities to International Investors

There are currently more than 35 equity markets in developing countries with a total market capitalization of almost $360 billion (as of September 1988), up from $67 billion five years ago (see Table 7.1) and more than 9,000 listings (See Table 7.2). Many of the larger emerging markets are comparable in size to the medium-sized European markets, although they are much smaller than New York or Japan.

There is much room for growth in these markets. Whereas the GNP of the countries with emerging markets contributes approximately 10 percent to world GNP, their financial markets still contribute less than 3 percent to world financial markets. Nevertheless, they have now reached a size and importance which can no longer be overlooked as demonstrated by the following examples:

In recent years equity and bond markets have mobilized more funds for development through new issues than have World Bank loan disbursements. In Korea and India alone, new issues exceeded $5 billion in 1985. The amounts mobilized by the financial markets in developing countries should continue to grow as market activity increases.

Many European markets have 100–500 listings, similar to the range found in most developing countries. More than 15 markets in the developing world have more than 100 companies. In India, more than 6,000 companies are listed, larger than markets in the United Kingdom and Japan, although most of these companies are much smaller and much less actively traded.

In recent years, there has been a boom in many emerging markets, especially various Asian markets. In 1987, of the top five performing markets, Taiwan, Korea, Thailand, and the Philippines placed first, second, third, and fifth. Japan was the fourth best performing market. In the first nine months of 1988, the top seven performing markets were from DCs (see Table 7.3).

As developing country markets become more active, as has been the case in recent years, new companies probably will list their shares, and the market capitalization of companies listed will grow. By the turn of the century, there could easily be 15,000 listings in the developing world, of which some 500 are to be traded in the international markets and held by institutional investors on a worldwide basis.

TABLE 7.1
Market Capitalization

(in US$ Millions)

	1986 Mar.	1986 Jun.	1986 Sep.	1986 Dec.	1987 Mar.	1987 Jun.	1987 Sep.	1987 Dec.	1988 Mar.	1988 Jun.	1988 Sep.
Latin America											
Argentina	1,734	2,165	1,810	1,591	1,918	1,584	1,622	1,519	1,375	1,893	2,733
Brazil (Sao Paulo)	77,803	76,147	48,569	42,096	19,815	20,799	23,415	16,900	25,177	26,535	30,211
Chile	2,580	2,695	3,027	4,062	4,699	4,414	6,172	5,341	5,684	6,484	6,606
Colombia	518	574	641	822	826	840	1,125	1,256	1,223	1,174	1,118
Mexico	4,040	4,500	4,680	5,950	10,691	18,814	37,100	12,674	17,668	20,221	21,180
Venezuela	-	-	-	-	-	-	-	2,278	2,623	2,091	1,626
East Asia											
Korea	9,216	11,514	12,114	13,924	21,404	23,396	27,836	32,905	42,612	57,472	63,009
Philippines	729	930	1,612	2,008	2,241	3,260	2,455	2,948	2,798	3,323	3,530
Taiwan, China	12,453	13,089	13,090	15,367	21,550	27,702	78,186	48,634	68,333	92,457	156,768
South Asia											
India (Bombay)	-	-	-	13,588	-	13,358	15,739	15,877	15,065	18,222	22,001
Malaysia	12,959	14,004	13,834	15,065	20,756	27,096	27,371	18,531	19,665	24,276	21,971
Pakistan	1,452	1,452	1,584	1,710	1,792	1,822	1,878	1,960	2,421	2,324	2,354
Thailand	1,797	1,848	2,282	2,878	3,233	4,525	7,136	5,485	7,629	9,514	9,666

Table 7.1, continued

	1986 Mar.	1986 Jun.	1986 Sep.	1986 Dec.	1987 Mar.	1987 Jun.	1987 Sep.	1987 Dec.	1988 Mar.	1988 Jun.	1988 Sep.
Europe•Mideast•Africa											
Greece	809	845	1,064	1,129	1,844	2,349	4,919	4,464	4,345	3,592	3,874
Jordan	2,457	2,525	2,600	2,839	2,672	2,448	2,505	2,643	2,559	2,473	2,414
Nigeria	2,979	2,680	2,150	1,112	1,069	1,166	1,001	974	1,014	1,059	1,083
Portugal	-	-	-	748	3,384	4,672	12,554	8,857	8,424	7,290	6,637
Turkey	-	-	-	935	1,323	2,353	4,680	3,221	2,468	1,720	1,473
Zimbabwe	388	389	407	410	438	488	547	718	789	723	712

*Estimated

Source: Quarterly Review of Emerging Stock Markets, Second Quarter 1988, Washington, D.C.: Capital Markets Department, International Finance Corporation, 1988, 6.

TABLE 7.2
Number of Listed Domestic Companies

	1980	1981	1982	1983	1984	1985	1986	1987
DEVELOPED MARKETS								
U.S.	6,251	6,866	6,834	7,722	7,977	8,022	8,403	7,181
U.K	2,655	2,403	2,279	2,217	2,171	2,116	2,106	2,135
Japan	1,402	1,412	1,427	1,441	1,444	1,829	2,549	1,912
Australia	1,007	982	931	930	1,009	1,028	1,162	1,528
Canada (Toronto)	731	771	759	808	943	912	1,034	1,147
S. Africa	481	475	470	464	470	462	536	838
France	586	568	535	518	504	489	482	650
Germany	459	456	450	442	449	472	492	507
Luxembourg	74	80	88	102	134	175	253	364
Spain (Madrid)	496	490	448	394	375	334	312	327
Israel	117	136	212	258	269	267	255	283
Denmark	218	219	206	211	231	243	274	277
Netherlands	214	202	216	215	263	232	219	248
Italy	134	132	138	138	143	147	184	204
Belgium	225	218	212	204	197	192	191	192
Switzerland (Zurich)	118	121	119	120	121	131	145	166
Sweden	103	130	138	145	159	164	154	157
Norway	117	109	112	113	140	156	149	146
Austria	66	63	62	62	63	64	74	69
	------	------	------	------	------	------	------	------
	15,454	15,833	15,636	16,504	17,062	17,435	18,974	18,331
EMERGING MARKETS								
India*	2,265	2,114	3,358	3,118	3,882	4,344	5,460	6,017
Brazil (Sao Paulo)	426	477	493	505	522	541	592	590
Korea	352	343	334	328	336	342	355	389
Pakistan	314	311	326	327	347	362	361	379
Mexico	271	240	215	174	178	188	166	233
Malaysia	182	187	194	204	217	222	223	232
Chile	265	242	212	214	208	228	231	209
Argentina	278	263	248	238	236	227	217	206
Portugal	25	23	26	25	23	24	40	143
Taiwan, China	102	107	113	119	123	127	130	141
Philippines (Manila)	194	196	201	195	150	138	128	138
Thailand	77	80	81	88	96	100	98	125
Greece	116	111	113	113	114	114	114	116
Venezuela	n.a.	n.a.	98	n.a.	116	108	108	110
Jordan	71	72	86	95	103	104	103	101
Nigeria	90	93	93	93	93	96	99	100
Colombia	n.a.	n.a.	193	196	180	102	99	96
Zimbabwe	62	62	62	60	56	55	53	53
Turkey	n.a.	n.a.	314	n.a.	373	n.a.	41	50
	------	------	------	------	------	------	------	------
	5,090	4,921	6,760	6,092	7,353	7,422	8,618	9,428
TOTAL	20,544	20,754	22,396	22,596	24,415	24,857	27,592	27,759

*Estimated

Source: Emerging Stock Markets Factbook 1988, Washington, D.C.: Capital Markets Department, International Finance Corporation, 1988, 38–39.

TABLE 7.3
Best Performing Markets, 1987 and 1988
(in U.S. Dollars)

	1987	(%)	1988	(%)
1.	Taiwan	182	Brazil	153
2.	Korea	108	Taiwan	123
3.	Zimbabwe	59	Korea	103
4.	Thailand	43	Mexico	93
5.	Japan	41	Argentina	92
6.	Philippines	36	Sweden	50
7.	South Africa	34	Thailand	36
8.	Spain	33	India	36
9.	United Kingdom	33	Japan	36
10.	Chile	15	Belgium	36
	U.S.A	.2		13

Source: Emerging Markets Investors Corporation, 1989.

Potential for International Investors

A major new phenomenon of the past few years is that international investors are showing an increasing interest in these emerging capital markets. Close to $1 billion has been invested by international institutions in Brazil, Korea, Taiwan, Malaysia, Mexico, and India. Investment flows could reach between $500 million and $1 billion a year by the 1990s if many of the remaining barriers to foreign portfolio investment are removed.

The current size of pension and investment funds is about $2.7 trillion. Only 1 percent of these funds would amount to $27 billion. The managers of these funds are looking worldwide for attractive returns, diversification, and good values, areas especially suited to emerging capital markets.

Attractive Returns

Many of the emerging markets have a respectable history of returns. Among ten of the top emerging markets tracked by the IFC Emerging Financial Markets Database since 1975 (see Table 7.4), Argentina, Chile, India, Korea, and Thailand have outperformed both the index for the industrialized world (Morgan Stanley — Capital International World Index) and the United States (S&P 500) over the past 11-year period. Mexico and Jordan, among others, are slightly below the international averages. Moreover, even with Black Monday, four of the top five performing markets in the world in 1987 were from emerging markets. Despite the debt crisis in the developing world and the recent boom in equity markets, the emerging markets have performed creditably in comparison over the most recent 11-year period.

Diversification

In addition to high returns for individual assets, institutional investors are also concerned with diversification of assets among different countries and industries, which will either increase return for a given level of risk or decrease risk for a given level of return. Risk for institutional investors is commonly referred to as the variance of returns or the standard deviation. In addition to returns, investors are concerned with the correlation between country markets. Ideally, when one market is down, another market should be doing well, which should offset the lower returns in the first market, lowering portfolio risk (i.e., variability). Correlation coefficients in many emerging markets with the United States and other industrialized markets are close to zero (see Table 7.5). This provides excellent diversification opportunities for international investors.

Good Values

Good values can be found in many emerging capital markets because they have not yet been discovered by international and local institutional investors, although a few of the markets may be temporarily overvalued.

Price-earnings and price/book value ratios are often well below the ratios in the major international markets (see Table 7.6). Because modern investment techniques and securities analysis are not yet used on a wide scale in these markets, comparative inefficiencies in these markets give international investors with the skills the opportunities to

TABLE 7.4
The IFC Emerging Markets Indexes[1] for Markets Followed since 1975 Cumulative Total Returns
(Based at Dec. 1975 = 100)

	1975	1976	1977	1978	1979	1980	1981	1982	1983	1984	1985	1986	1987
Latin America													
Argentina	100	563	273	741	2,653	2,504	1,346	524	776	651	1,138	837	920
Brazil	100	99	90	75	53	51	69	59	92	142	277	210	78
Chile	100	207	489	770	1,773	3,224	1,861	846	579	442	660	1,682	2,242
Mexico	100	77	97	201	349	358	194	49	98	111	131	262	239
Asia													
India	100	130	145	200	234	322	417	407	413	401	823	800	677
Korea	100	180	370	457	398	307	435	449	436	531	736	1,385	1,940
Thailand	100	109	260	376	261	244	205	277	339	335	342	615	848
Europe, Mideast, Africa													
Greece	100	106	132	135	123	89	61	61	29	24	25	39	97
Jordan	-	-	100	147	199	239	364	359	334	293	435	419	400
Zimbabwe	100	81	78	65	153	209	77	44	39	37	93	110	215
Developed Markets													
MS-CI, World	100	115	117	138	156	199	193	214	264	279	396	566	660
USA, S&P 500	100	124	114	122	144	191	182	221	271	288	379	449	472
Japan Nikkei Dow	100	125	144	219	193	249	287	264	329	384	548	1,089	1,604

[1]Converted to U.S. Dollars at the end of each period.
[2]The Amman Financial market began operations on January 1, 1978.
MS–CI = Morgan Stanley–Capital International

Source: Emerging Stock Markets, 10.

TABLE 7.5

Correlation Coefficient Matrix of Changes of Price Indexes

(5 Years Ending September 1988)

	USA	JPN	ARG	BRA	CHI	COL	GRE	IND	JOR	KOR	MAL	MEX	NIG	PAK	PHI	POR	TAI	THA	TUR	VEN	ZIM
USA	1.00																				
JPN	0.08	1.00																			
ARG	-0.01	-0.01	1.00																		
BRA	0.04	-0.01	0.15	1.00																	
CHI	0.27	-0.12	0.02	-0.12	1.00																
COL	0.14	0.02	-0.12	-0.14	0.32	1.00															
GRE	0.26	-0.06	-0.01	-0.31	0.27	0.43	1.00														
IND	0.02	0.07	0.10	-0.06	-0.05	-0.11	-0.01	1.00													
JOR	-0.16	-0.01	-0.01	0.10	-0.07	-0.12	0.07	0.43	1.00												
KOR	0.30	-0.10	0.14	0.06	0.17	0.10	0.01	0.01	-0.28	1.00											
MAL	0.51	0.07	-0.03	0.15	0.27	-0.12	0.08	-0.03	-0.11	-0.02	1.00										
MEX	0.31	0.09	-0.05	0.03	0.44	0.13	0.16	-0.01	-0.15	0.16	0.40	1.00									
NIG	0.15	0.14	0.11	-0.13	0.07	0.10	0.03	0.03	-0.07	0.10	-0.25	-0.14	1.00								
PAK	-0.14	-0.05	0.06	0.03	0.10	0.17	0.10	0.15	0.29	0.01	-0.20	0.13	-0.01	1.00							
PHI	0.16	-0.15	-0.15	-0.11	0.25	-0.02	0.03	-0.07	-0.13	0.17	0.25	0.04	0.15	-0.02	1.00						
POR	0.18	0.01	-0.14	0.00	0.26	0.39	0.53	-0.19	0.04	-0.06	0.20	0.39	-0.22	0.17	-0.17	1.00					
TAI	0.09	0.10	-0.10	0.09	0.30	0.16	0.24	-0.10	-0.18	-0.17	0.18	0.43	-0.21	0.07	-0.23	0.53	1.00				
THA	0.31	0.02	0.05	0.02	0.33	0.16	0.35	-0.02	0.04	-0.10	0.49	0.43	-0.18	0.22	0.04	0.40	0.56	1.00			
TUR	0.35	0.05	-0.14	-0.06	0.27	0.18	0.09	-0.05	-0.28	0.27	0.40	0.37	0.05	0.10	0.36	0.34	0.11	0.24	1.00		
VEN	-0.07	0.13	-0.08	-0.05	-0.18	-0.03	-0.08	-0.10	0.24	-0.18	0.17	0.00	0.02	0.07	-0.02	0.07	-0.11	0.05	0.26	1.00	
ZIM	-0.13	-0.09	-0.18	-0.07	0.04	-0.10	0.18	0.16	0.25	-0.20	-0.03	-0.06	-0.01	0.29	0.03	0.19	-0.11	0.01	-0.03	0.13	1.00
	USA	JPN	ARG	BRA	CHI	COL	GRE	IND	JOR	KOR	MAL	MEX	NIG	PAK	PHI	POR	TAI	THA	TUR	VEN	ZIM

Source: Quarterly Review, 18.

TABLE 7.6
Comparative Valuations

	Valuations at September 30, 1988			Valuation Relative to MS-CI World*		
	Price Earnings(x)	Price/Book Value(x)	Dividend Yield(%)	Price Earnings(x)	Price/Book Value(x)	Dividend Yield(%)
Developed Markets						
Germany	14.7	1.8	3.7	0.8	0.8	1.5
France	11.4	1.6	3.2	0.7	0.7	1.3
Japan	51.9	4.6	0.5	3.0	2.0	0.2
U.K.	10.6	1.8	5.0	0.6	0.8	2.0
U.S.A.	11.8	1.8	3.7	0.7	0.8	1.5
World	17.3	2.3	2.5	1.0	1.0	1.0
Latin America						
Argentina	9.8	1.0	2.1	0.6	0.4	0.8
Brazil	4.6	0.6	3.3	0.3	0.2	1.3
Chile	5.1	1.0	8.7	0.3	0.5	3.5
Colombia	8.0	1.4	6.5	0.5	0.6	2.6
Mexico	5.6	0.8	3.8	0.3	0.3	1.5
Venezuela	12.5	2.8	1.1	0.7	1.2	0.5
East Asia						
Korea	36.8	2.5	0.7	2.1	1.1	0.3
Philippines	9.6	2.5	2.4	0.6	1.1	1.0
Taiwan, China	46.5	6.8	0.4	2.7	3.0	0.1
South Asia						
India	33.3	3.1	2.6	1.9	1.3	1.0
Malaysia	22.6	2.4	1.5	1.3	1.0	0.6
Pakistan	9.3	1.6	3.0	0.5	0.7	1.2
Thailand	13.6	4.2	3.0	0.8	1.8	1.2

Europe•Mideast•Africa

Greece	11.1	2.4	5.5	0.6	1.0	2.2
Jordan	14.0	1.2	6.5	0.8	0.5	2.6
Nigeria	6.2	3.4	6.7	0.4	1.5	2.7
Portugal	26.9	4.4	0.8	1.6	1.9	0.3
Turkey	7.8	2.8	8.8	0.5	1.2	3.5
Zimbabwe	1.7	4.2	9.1	0.1	1.8	3.6

*MS–CI = Morgan Stanley–Capital International.

Source: Quarterly Review, 6.

find values no longer to be found through existing methods in the major markets.

Some of the world industry leaders can be found in many developing countries. Many exporters to the industrialized world are quoted on local stock markets in the developing world. The demand for protection against their products is evidence of the threat they pose to competitors elsewhere.

Many emerging capital markets are in countries with economies fundamentally sounder than they were five or ten years ago. Many are benefitting from the recent alignment in major international currencies. Others are becoming more private-sector oriented, have abandoned overvalued exchange rates, and have trimmed the fat of their corporate sectors during the recent shake-up of their economies.

Potential Problems: Myth or Reality

The appeal of investing in emerging markets is clear. Why has it not happened on a wider scale? The most important barrier in the past has been the lack of knowledge and information among international investors about the emerging capital markets. Investors thought that these markets were small; lacking liquidity; without significant disclosure, information, and investor protection; restricted for foreigners; and politically risky. Some of these problems do indeed exist but perhaps on a smaller scale than expected.

Liquidity. On the whole, emerging markets are not very liquid in the sense that major blocks of stocks can be sold and bought without major price movements. However, liquidity on many of these markets is comparable to that on the smaller European exchanges (see Table 7.7). It should also be remembered that there are only about 100 stocks in the United States generally considered very liquid. In the week of Black Monday, institutional investors found it quite difficult to trade many of the smaller NASDAQ stocks.

Disclosure. Disclosure in most emerging markets is not comparable to practices in the United States but is often surprisingly good if compared with that of many companies listed in Europe and Japan. A sizable number of companies quoted in the major emerging markets are audited by subsidiaries of large European and U.S. accounting firms.

Information. Information on most emerging markets is becoming increasingly available (see Table 7.8). The IFC has a commercially available database covering the top 18 markets in detail. It supplies aggregates, price indices, and other relevant data for investors. Daily price quotations are now available on Reuters screens in more than 15 of the major emerging markets. Most of the major stock markets in developing countries have available a wealth of stock market statistics, even company data. And several brokerage firms are now publishing regular reports on various Pacific markets and companies.

Securities Legislation. Many, but not all, of the major emerging markets have securities legislation patterned after U.S. securities laws, or, in a few cases, British laws. However, enforcement of investor protection and sanctions against insider protection are sometimes lax.

Investment Restrictions. Although there are indeed investment restrictions in most developing countries, the trend is clearly toward gradual liberalization and internationalization of the markets. Among the top markets, Malaysia, Chile, Thailand, and the Philippines are already relatively open. Brazil, India, Taiwan, and Korea are now accessible through a variety of funds. In Mexico, a limited number of individual shares can be purchased (see Table 7.9). The most specific program of liberalization is in place in Korea. Signs in other countries indicate that they also may be opening up to international investors.

Taxes. In most of these countries, withholding taxes are close to the international average or are likely to be brought in line very soon (see Table 7.10). In Chile and Malaysia, however, a heavy withholding tax on dividends has replaced a corporate income tax. Further improvement and liberalization clearly are needed, but investment restrictions are no longer a major reason for avoiding emerging markets.[1]

Interest of International Equities to DC Investors

Just as international investors find developing country equity of interest because of attractive returns, diversification, and good values, the same benefits accrue to developing country investors through including a few international assets in the local investors' considered set. However, DC governments have gradually opened equity markets for additional reasons. In Taiwan, the markets were gradually opened to allow investors on a limited basis to purchase international security as a means to reduce the large trade surplus with developed countries. In Brazil, 1401 funds were allowed to tap additional international funds in forms other than bank debt. Although returns in developed countries are not usually as high as in developing countries, likewise, the risks of international securities, on the whole, tend to be less than of DC equity.

TABLE 7.7
Value Traded

(In US$ Millions)

	1980	1981	1982	1983	1984	1985	1986	1987
DEVELOPED MARKETS								
U.S.A.	409,816	415,760	508,144	797,123	786,204	997,189	1,795,998	2,423,066
Japan	180,204	255,710	165,220	266,061	338,589	382,525	1,097,894	2,047,224
U.K.	35,791	32,542	32,676	42,544	48,857	68,417	132,912	389,829
Germany	15,248	13,670	14,490	32,949	29,764	71,572	135,700	373,428
France	10,118	8,403	7,328	8,345	7,690	14,672	51,548	88,085
Canada	28,211	23,430	16,411	28,444	25,822	39,905	56,810	75,189
Australia	9,556	7,935	5,123	9,320	10,654	15,736	26,871	58,860
Hong Kong	19,226	18,959	7,615	5,116	6,243	9,732	15,299	47,627
Netherlands	5,099	3,978	4,837	10,182	12,274	16,864	31,122	39,542
Spain	981	1,622	1,380	1,300	2,465	3,382	14,944	36,070
Italy	8,574	10,850	2,787	3,872	4,065	13,782	44,715	32,379
Sweden	1,796	3,669	4,614	9,847	8,496	9,644	19,830	19,588
Austria	105	84	73	133	114	686	1,393	9,754
S. Africa	5,129	2,837	2,575	3,752	2,528	2,836	4,990	9,568
Norway	84	101	96	962	1,350	1,877	1,702	8,935
Belgium	838	643	1,062	1,432	1,575	1,876	4,343	7,148
Singapore	3,654	6,377	2,419	5,588	3,849	1,383	2,679	6,854
Israel	2,447	4,210	6,650	10,284	735	748	1,455	4,828
Denmark	58	59	56	181	173	1,274	1,866	1,913
Luxembourg	19	17	17	17	22	36	109	111
Sub-total	736,956	810,857	783,572	1,237,449	1,291,470	1,654,136	3,442,181	5,680,000

EMERGING MARKETS

Taiwan, China	4,503	5,677	3,422	9,081	8,194	4,899	18,931	84,112
Korea	1,867	3,721	2,700	2,260	3,869	4,162	10,889	24,919
Mexico	2,749	3,663	660	1,110	2,106	4,403	6,049	16,709
Brazil	5,383	6,185	5,938	4,884	9,960	21,485	28,912	9,608
Thailand	308	108	238	381	434	568	1,133	4,633
Malaysia	2,572	3,498	1,392	3,398	2,226	2,335	1,180	3,829
India	2,760	7,386	5,030	2,377	3,916	4,959	10,032	2,862
Philippines	619	163	142	483	125	111	563	1,524
Portugal	2	2	1	1	3	5	82	1,518
Chile	548	375	163	65	51	57	298	503
Greece	86	55	37	17	12	17	32	441
Jordan	139	227	318	329	138	163	185	420
Argentina	1,089	454	231	389	277	631	309	251
Pakistan	n.a.	n.a.	n.a.	n.a.	n.a.	n.a.	155	162
Venezuela	60	47	82	59	27	31	52	148
Turkey	n.a.	n.a.	n.a.	n.a.	n.a.	n.a.	13	122
Colombia	187	332	93	65	47	30	49	80
Zimbabwe	154	136	75	38	6	9	12	23
Nigeria	14	10	12	18	16	15	16	7
Sub-total	23,041	32,039	20,535	24,955	31,407	43,879	78,893	151,871
TOTAL	759,996	842,896	804,107	1,262,404	1,322,877	1,698,016	3,521,073	5,831,871

Source: *Emerging Stock Markets*, 34–35.

TABLE 7.8
Access to Market Information and Investor Protection

	Share Price Index	(1) Securities Exchange Bulletin	(2) Regular Publication of P/E, Yield	(3) Market Commentaries in English by Brokerage Houses	(4) Company Stock Reports	(5) Disclosure Requirements Accounting Standards	(6) Investor Protection	(7) International Electronic Coverage
LATIN AMERICA								
Argentina	X	M, Q, A	P	–	–	A	A S	X
Brazil	X	M, A	C	AR	AR	G	G S	X
Chile	X	M, Q, A	C	LR	LR, IR	G	G S	X
Colombia	X	M, Q, A	P	AR	LR, IR	A	A S	X
Mexico	X	M, A	C	IR AR	AR	G	G S	X
Venezuela	X	M, Q, A	P	AR	LR	A	A S	X
ASIA								
India	X	A, W	P	LR	LR	G	G S	X
Indonesia	X	A	–	LR AR	–	A	P S	–
Korea	X	M, A	C	IR	IR	G	G S	X
Malaysia	X	M, A	C	IR	AR	G	G –	X
Pakistan	X	A	P	AR	AR	A	A S	–
Philippines	X	M, A	C	LR	LR, AR	G	A S	X
Taiwan, China	X	M, A	P	LR, AR	LR, IR	P	P S	X
Thailand	X	M, A	C	LR, AR	LR, AR	A	A S	X

EUROPE, MIDDLE EAST, AFRICA

		(1)	(2)	(3) & (4)		(5) & (6)			
Greece	X	M, A	–	–	AR	A	P	–	X
Ivory Coast	–	A	–	–	AR	P	A	–	X
Jordan	X	A, M, W	P	AR	AR*	P	A	S	X
Kenya	X	A	–	LR	AR	P	P	–	–
Morocco	X	A	–	–	AR	A	P	–	–
Nigeria	X	A	–	AR	AR	G	A	S	X
Portugal	X	A, Q, M	P	–	AR	P	A	S	X
Turkey	X	M, A	P	–	–	A	P	S	X
Zimbabwe	X	A	P	LR	LR	A	A	S	–

KEY

Column	Symbol	
(1)	A	= Annual, Q = Quarterly, M = Monthly, W = Weekly
(2)	C	= Comprehensive and published internationally, P = published
(3) & (4)	LR	= Prepared by local brokers or international manager
	IR	= Prepared by international manager/broker
	AR	= Annual Report of Securities Exchange
	*	= in local language only
(5) & (6)	G	= Good, of internationally acceptable quality; A = Adequate; P = Poor, requires reform.
	S	= Functioning Securities Commission or similar government agency concentrating on regulating market activity.

Source: Emerging Stock Markets, 42–43.

TABLE 7.9
Entering and Exiting Emerging Markets — Investment Restrictions*

(At Year-End 1987)

	Repatriation of:	
Free Entry	**Income**	**Capital**
Malaysia	Free	Free
Portugal	Some Restrictions	Free
Kenya	Restricted	Some Restrictions
Philippines	Some Restrictions	Only after 3 months
Jordan	Free	Free
Relatively Free	**Repatriation of:**	
Entry	**Income**	**Capital**
Thailand	Some Restrictions	Some Restrictions
Chile	Some Restrictions	Only after 5 years
Argentina	Restricted	Only after 3 years
Colombia	Some Restrictions	Free
Mexico	Some Restrictions	Some Restrictions
Restricted to	**Repatriation by Funds of:**	
Special Funds	**Income**	**Capital**
Brazil	Free	Only after 3 months
Korea	Free	Only on Fund liquidation
Taiwan, China	Once per year	Free
India	Free	Free
Restricted by	**Repatriation of:**	
Investor Nationality	**Income**	**Capital**
India — Non-Resident Indians only	Free	Free
Pakistan — Non-Resident Pakistanis only	Only after 1 year	Only after 1 year
Greece	Free to EEC Nationals	Free to EEC Nationals
Restricted by	**Repatriation of:**	
Shares	**Income**	**Capital**
Zimbabwe — only shares not already quoted on foreign markets	Restricted	Only after 2 years, with other restrictions
Venezuela — only shares held by non-residents or shares arising from new issues or capital increases.	Restricted	Restricted

continued

Table 7.9, continued

Closed or Severely Restricted	Repatriation of: Income	Capital
Nigeria	Access not contemplated in current laws.	
Indonesia	Access not contemplated in current laws.	
Turkey	Allowed upon SPO authorization.	

Key: Income = dividends, interest, and realized capital gains. Some restrictions = Typically, requires registration with or permission of Central Bank, Ministry of Finance or an Office of Exchange Controls. Free = Repatriation done routinely.

*It should also be noted that some industries in some countries are considered strategic and are not available to foreign/non-resident investors, and that the level of foreign investment in other cases may be limited by national law or corporate policy to minority positions not to aggregate more than 49 percent of voting stock.

Source: Emerging Stock Markets, 47.

Implications of Equity Market Integration

Internationalizing equity markets in developing countries has important implications for international investors, DC investors, industrialized country governments, and developing country governments.

To international investors, developing country stocks may be of interest to international portfolio managers because of their higher returns, low covariances with developed country markets, and relatively good values. Moreover, the size of the equity markets in relation to their total GNP and the current economic growth rates of DCs as compared to developed countries gives reason to believe that the markets are currently underdeveloped and may have room to grow. Not including these in the considered set of assets may reduce the return and increase the risk of the international investor's portfolio.

To developing country investors, there may be both a domestic and an international market for developing country stocks. The current size of the pool of international pension and investment funds looking for good investment opportunities makes it a viable source to be tapped, should local markets be opened for investment. The willingness of international investors to own well-run DC stocks sold on the U.S. and London exchanges in the form of depositary receipts also can add to the visibility, name recognition, and liquidity of DC companies.

Including some international stocks (either bought internationally or on the local exchange) in a DC company's portfolio may increase return or decrease risk through diversification. If government regulations permit, some well-capitalized and regularly traded domestic firms should look to the international market as another and possibly cheaper source of raising funds for operations. Listing firms in more than one market often results in a lower cost of equity capital for DC firms. An additional side benefit is that to gain international recognition, improving the amount of information to the international investing public is necessary.

Industrialized country governments also reap benefits from investing in developing countries. Some of the current problems of the debt crisis in DCs would not have occurred had the countries financed the private projects through issuing equity. Not only would investors have been more careful with the planning but also projects would have been evaluated with a more critical eye to the repayment probabilities of each

TABLE 7.10
Withholding Taxes for U.S.-Based Institutional Investors
(Percentage Rates in Effect at the End of 1987)

	Interest %	Dividends %	Long-Term Capital Gains On Listed Shares %
LATIN AMERICA			
ARGENTINA	15.75	17.5	45
BRAZIL	25	15	none
CHILE	35	40[2] [5]	40[3]
COLOMBIA	40	20	15
MEXICO	21	55[5]	none
VENEZUELA	15	none[1]	none[1]
EUROPE, MIDDLE EAST			
GREECE	none	42[5]	none
JORDAN	none	none	none
PORTUGAL	15	12	none
TURKEY	10	25	none
AFRICA			
COTE D'IVOIRE	18	12	none
KENYA	12.5	7.5	11
MOROCCO	22	15	none
NIGERIA	40	15	20
ZIMBABWE	10	20	30

continued

TABLE 7.10, continued

ASIA				
INDIA[6]	25	25	40
INDONESIA	20	20	none
KOREA[4]	12.9	16.125	none
MALAYSIA	20 (0%)	40 (0%)	none
PAKISTAN	55	15	none
PHILIPPINES	15	25	0.25[7]
TAIWAN, CHINA[8]	20	20	none
THAILAND	15 (10%)	25 (10%)	10

(Rates shown in brackets apply only to Country Funds, where these are different from normal treatment).

[1]Rates apply only to shares of publicly controlled companies (SAICA).

[2]None if reinvested; 40 percent withheld otherwise (with offsetting 10 percent tax credit).

[3]Gains above inflation.

[4]Rate under tax treaty with the United States.

[5]Unlike the other countries listed, Mexico, Greece and Chile have no corporate profit tax on distributed earnings.

[6]Rate for Non-Resident Indian Portfolio Investors; rates on foreign direct investment are higher.

[7]Rate applies to gross sale proceeds.

[8]Available only to investors in approved investment vehicles.

Source: Emerging Stock Markets, 51.

project. The ability of firms to finance projects through equity capital and local debt financing may reduce the amounts of international borrowing.

In addition, because of the high returns and low correlations with industrialized markets, industrialized governments, which have too stringent requirements regarding the allowance of prudent pension fund investment in developing countries, may actually be detrimental to industrialized country firms. Because of the lower returns and higher risks from not including DC stocks, pension and other funds will require greater company contributions because of lower returns from investments.

For developing country governments, there are three major implications. First, foreign portfolio investment, at least from a U.S. dollar numeraire, may be a viable alternative source of funds for development. Because of the higher returns and the low correlations with the U.S. market, developing country stocks are viable investment candidates for foreign investors. By not allowing foreign investors to purchase developing country stocks, government officials are eliminating a possible source of funds for private-sector development.

Second, the ability of domestic portfolios to gain yield at the same risk (or reduce risk without a change in yield) by judiciously including foreign assets could help private sector growth in developing countries (e.g., by reducing the firm's contribution to pension funds because the higher yield would offset lower firm contribution). Thus, by not allowing developing country investors to invest a small portion of assets in international securities (by allowing either a few international firms to list locally or local firms to purchase international securities) private-sector return may be reduced. Allowing a small number of international stocks to be traded in the domestic market may increase returns and lower risk to domestic investors. This could have an important effect on reducing the cost of pension fund and life insurance schemes in developing countries. Recall the work of Subrahmanyam indicating that lowering barriers to two-way investment fund flows across borders would benefit citizens of both countries.[2]

INTERMEDIARY STEPS TO INTERNATIONALIZATION OF THE MARKETS

When discussing international investment in developing countries, many individuals often think of full liberalization of portfolio investment and the ability of foreigners to invest immediately in those markets. Although this is a good objective for most developing countries, there are intermediary steps toward this objective. These steps have been successful in mobilizing additional funds for development, which may not have as large an effect on DCs as immediate full liberalization. This final section discusses intermediary steps for developing countries that are considering the gradual opening of their markets. This includes investment by international investors in multinational corporations (MNCs) with activities in the DC, allowing nonresident citizens to invest in local equities, foreign depositary receipts, country funds, and convertible bonds. Once the country has the time and experience to evaluate and understand the implication of opening the market to foreign investment (and also allowing domestic investors to invest internationally), the final step may be opening the market to foreign investors.

Indirect Investment in Multinational Corporations

Much has been written regarding investing in MNCs or in foreign equities to obtain the greatest diversification potential. Most research has found higher diversification opportunities in investing in foreign securities. However, when local markets are closed to foreign investment, often the only alternative is investing in MNCs with large operations in the developing country. The assumption is that because the MNC has operations in the developing country and because a percentage of company returns are correlated with the overall economy, the returns of the MNC will mirror the returns in the market. Special funds have been developed for China that invest only in those companies doing business in China.

As a diversification technique, MNCs have been found not to be extensively affected by foreign factors and behave much like the stock price of a purely domestic firm. Reasons include the importance of national control, accounting considerations, government constraints, and the influence of major stock markets where the stock is traded. Regardless of the limitations, in some developing countries, investing in MNCs is the only available proxy to foreign portfolio investment.

Allowing Nonresident DC Citizens to Invest in Equities

Some countries, such as India, allow nonresident citizens to invest in the local equity markets. This policy may be beneficial because it constitutes an additional source of funds for investment. Distinction is made between residents and nonresidents, with limitations placed on the type and amount of ownership allowed by nonresident citizens. These regulations ensure that nonresident investors have some ties to the local economy but do not allow them to have a controlling position with local companies. An added benefit from allowing nonresident citizens to invest is that remittances may also be a source of needed foreign currency.

Foreign Depositary Receipts

Foreign depositary receipts are negotiable receipts created by banks to facilitate trading of securities issued by companies from outside the domestic market. They are used because companies often outgrow their domestic markets or face limitations to their long-term funding because of local market conditions. International Depositary Receipts (IDRs) or

American Depositary Receipts (ADRs) have been issued for companies from many developing countries, including the Philippines, Malaysia, Liberia, Mexico, and Zimbabwe. Companies from other countries also are considering the issuance of shares.

ADRs or IDRs are beneficial to developing countries because they offer an additional source of funds for development without concern for destabilizing capital flows, allow a greater name recognition by international investors, and broaden the company's investor base. ADRs and IDRs are beneficial to international investors because they allow greater diversification. ADRs mirror local markets, have all financial statements and other information translated into the local language, and have dividends converted into the local currency, thereby minimizing time and expense.

Country Funds

An additional successful intermediary step to liberalization has been issuing country funds. Many developing countries have restricted foreign portfolio investors from investing in individual stocks but have allowed investment in country funds. Funds have been established in Korea, Brazil, Taiwan, Mexico, India, and Brazil. Others are under discussion. These funds introduce unfamiliar countries to the international investment community and create an appetite for individual stock and bond issues from these countries. Many of the recent offerings have been closed-end funds — their capital base is fixed — instead of open-end funds, such as mutual funds. In addition to country funds, many Hong Kong and London based investment managers offer regional Far Eastern Funds, and the IFC recently raised $50 million for an Emerging Market Growth Fund to invest in 20 developing countries. Many of these funds have done very well, with shares trading at a premium over net asset value.

In addition to single country funds, some DCs, such as Korea, have allowed limited direct investment in the stock exchanges through several mutual funds created for foreign investors as a step toward liberalizing and internationalizing the market. However, problems sometimes exist, such as in the case of the Taiwan fund, where there was an attempt to invest a large volume of equity in a relatively small market. Although there has been considerable success in issuing country funds, the amounts invested have been a very small percentage of total market capitalization in each country.

Convertible Bonds

As another step toward internationalizing the markets, some countries have allowed corporations, such as Korea's Samsung Electronics Company, Ltd., to issue quasi-equity instruments, such as bonds convertible to common stock. Because of the convertibility feature, interest requirements are much lower, lowering the company's overall cost of capital. In addition, should the convertibility feature be exercised, the need for the interest payment is eliminated and the investor base has been broadened. Moreover, interest paid on common stocks comes from after-tax earnings whereas interest paid on bonds is a tax-deductible expense.

For prospective investors, a convertible bond from a DC company has a number of advantages. First, although at a lower rate of interest than for a nonconvertible bond, it usually offers a regular fixed payment in a major currency, instead of irregular dividends in the local currency. Second, because they have a fixed maturity date, they must be redeemed unless converted. The approaching maturity date may protect the investor against a possible decline in the stock price. Third, the denomination in a major currency protects the investor from much of the exchange risk. And fourth, the conversion feature adds to the marketability of the issue.

Restricted International Investment

Some countries, such as Thailand, allow international investors to invest in selected companies up to a stated legal amount, usually 49 percent of company ownership. This allows countries to obtain the benefits of international funding without the concerns that the companies are controlled by foreigners. These shares are sold on a special exchange for international investors only. Because of the attractiveness of these companies and the limitations on ownership, international shares sometimes trade at a premium reflecting their scarcity to the international public.

Full Internationalization of the Markets

Many countries, such as Singapore and Hong Kong, allow international investors to invest fully in these markets. There are few distinctions between local and international investors, and many firms are listed on more than one exchange. Although the markets differ in the amount of regulation, they have been successful in mobilizing billions of dollars of both domestic and international funds to aid in individual company expansion and overall country economic development.

NOTES

1. For a more quantitative analysis of the advantages of international diversification into developing countries using actual stocks from DCs rather than indexes, see Sudweeks and Anckonie, 1987.

2. Subrahmanyam, "Optimality," 3–28.

8

Suggestions for Equity Market Development

Equity markets are a component in the network of capital flows in an economy.[1] In order to facilitate the creation of equity markets, one must first understand the total process of capital mobilization that takes place as industries develop from one stage of economic growth to another, in the context of a free market economy.

CAPITAL MOBILIZATION

In general the channels of financial flows evolve in the following pattern: self-financing, including sole proprietorships and cottage industries; early external financing, including informal (kerb) market loans, bank loans with collateral, and venture capital and partnerships; and mature financing, including debt in various forms (bank loans with or without collateral and borrowing in capital markets, domestic or foreign), equity in various forms (private placement of stocks for private corporations), public placement of stocks in the primary market, either domestic or foreign, and active trading of stocks in the secondary market, either domestic or foreign.

These three stages in the capital mobilization process are not discrete, and not one of them is present exclusively in any one country. For example, in the United States we find a variety of financial arrangements such as self-financed craft industries, large privately held corporations, and small publicly traded stocks.

However, even though the sophistication and depth of each stage in the financial process may vary widely, every stage is driven by one common force: private initiative. Without private initiative in a free market environment, the channels of distribution of financial resources become clogged and overflow into actions detrimental to the economy. A prime example is distortions in interest rates and foreign exchange that cause domestic savings to transform into capital flight.

It may appear that the conclusion is to remove controls from the marketplace and allow market forces to find their natural course toward economic growth. However, this conclusion is incorrect because the goal is to achieve not only economic growth in terms of output of goods and services but also economic growth that fosters a higher standard of living. In this context, a certain degree of government intervention is required.

Pitfalls of the Free Market

Free markets foster the efficient, but not always equitable, allocation of resources in the economy. When efficiency drives the market, financial resources gravitate only toward those investments that offer a reward above the required return adjusted for risk. In the strictest sense, inefficient projects are purged from the market. Unfortunately, among those projects there may be infant industries unable to benefit from economies of scale or social projects whose yield cannot be measured or rewarded in financial terms.

There is also difficult adaptation from an environment protected by regulation to a rigorously competitive arena. A sudden change to deregulation can make companies insolvent and the labor force vulnerable to uncertainties too hard to bear until the benefits of the free market are felt. The result is political unrest and return by new leadership to the old system or even more severe protective regulations than before.

Pitfalls of a Controlled Market

The undesirable traits of the free market system can be corrected by regulation. However, excessive government intervention becomes counterproductive. Usually, governments are reluctant to terminate or reform popular laws and programs regardless of how unreasonable they might be from an economic standpoint. As a result, governments subsidize socially and economically unproductive projects. Without the free-market price mechanism to purge unproductive projects from the market, governments continue to perpetuate costly projects that produce more burdens than benefits.

A Delicate Balance

Governments must intervene in the marketplace to ensure the achievement of national goals as well as equity in economic development, but they must also be prepared to relinquish controls that block the natural course of private enterprise.

The right course of action then is to find the delicate balance of private initiative and flexible government regulation that builds a solid foundation for long-term growth conducive to a higher standard of living.

The key to this concept is balance and flexibility meaning just the right kind of government regulation at the right time with enough flexibility to respond to changing circumstances.

Neither extreme of oppressive government restrictions or uncontrolled business practices is healthy. Rather, government and business activities must complement each other. The ideal situation has governments providing the appropriate business environment while business spearheads economic development.

Environment for Equity Market Development

Government regulation may permeate the whole financial system, not to restrict but rather to facilitate an environment where the private sector flourishes. Contrary to popular belief, the driving force behind successful financial development programs has been private-sector initiative.

In the case of equity markets, it has been proven that neither markets nor investment instruments can be legislated into existence. The initiative of private investors creates the market and determines the suitability of investments. However, this fact does not diminish the role of governments. On the contrary, their role becomes all the more vital because governments must provide an environment where instruments can compete equally and where trades among investors are conducted fairly.

A fine line divides official and private responsibilities, hence the importance of defining them in order to avoid encroachment by either side. For example, even though governments must enforce rules against market rigging and price inflation, they should abstain from fixing the price of new instruments and expressing views that might bias the market. Governments must allow stock exchanges to exercise a good measure of self-regulation but, at the same time, must guard against fraud and deceit in the form of misrepresentation, improper disclosure, and unfair practices.

In essence, market assessment and price determination are the realm of private buyers and sellers. Creation of appropriate environments is the role of governments.

Some important facts must be kept in mind in the process of facilitating equity market development. Equity market activity is basically a private-sector activity carried out by investors, issuers, and securities professionals as a result of their perceptions of risk and reward. This activity is imbued with the public interest and must conform to norms for the public's well-being. However, governments wishing to develop their markets should not repeat the error of other countries by ignoring the private sector and simply attempting to fashion a government-imposed system.

In designing the exchange systems and rules and regulations, the thrust must come from the private sector, and the participants must, with the government, select a system compatible to both. The government should not start with the view that the private sector is not involved or that private-sector expertise is lacking. Numerous development programs have failed, or have been seriously impeded, because the government dominated the process and distrusted the private sector. Removing this attitude is one of the most important contributions to a development goal.

Equity markets, like all financial markets, are dynamic. They are constantly changing to meet differing patterns of savings, fiscal conditions, institutional arrangements, and the supply and demand for funds. As opportunities and conditions change, that is, as the risk-adjusted yield of instruments varies through time, investors accommodate these developments by devising new strategies. Consequently, the overall goal of any development program should not be to specify in minute detail every aspect of a fixed and rigid financial system; it should be to establish a system that is flexible enough to meet new market conditions and the needs of market participants over time.

FINANCIAL SYSTEM DEVELOPMENT

Developing a single universal pattern of equity market development for all countries is difficult because all nations have different histories, cultures, governments, and natural resource endowments. However, despite the lack of uniformity among nations and the dynamic nature of changing markets, important basic steps should be taken regardless of differences. These steps should be of special interest to many developing countries who are actively seeking to develop their equity markets in order to encourage domestic savings and to mobilize these savings for productive use. Because equity market development must be part of an overall program for financial market development, this section proposes a framework for equity market development, including seven components usually present in a financial system development program in developing countries. These include analysis of the present financial system; development of a medium- and long-term strategy of financial market development in light of the social, economic, and political objectives of the country; design of a legislative and policy framework, especially fiscal and monetary policy to meet the overall country objectives; construction of a system of governmental overview and regulation of financial institutions and markets; training and development of an adequate supply of personnel for both the public and private sectors; implementation of a system of public and private accounting and auditing, together with rules on financial disclosure; and development of an appropriate range of public and private financial instruments, as well as markets, institutions, and services.

Equity market development is normally equated with only the last component of the development program. However, as discussed below, equity market development (or the development of the environment conducive to the development of an equity market) must include each of the seven components.

Current Financial System Analysis

The first major component of any financial system development program is a thorough analysis of the present strengths and weaknesses of the current financial system to determine the need for financial system development. This analysis is usually entrusted to multilateral, bilateral, or private consulting groups such as the Capital Markets Department of International Finance Corporation (World Bank Group), the U.S. Agency for International Development, or in-house consultants. The advantage of using independent consultants is that they contribute a variety of differing viewpoints and add objectivity to the process. This type of assessment is a valuable first step in any new program. It is also an important evaluation tool that should be used regularly — at least every five years — to ensure that development is consistent with the goals and long-term objectives of the developing country.

Areas to be covered in this analysis include the major areas discussed in this book: the economic and political environment; the legislative, institution, and regulatory framework; the interest rate, exchange rate, taxation, institutional investors, and foreign participation policies; the current supply, demand, and ownership of securities; primary and secondary markets; and other related areas such as informal markets, leasing, and venture capital. This is a methodical analysis of the existing financial system in the country with an emphasis on current system strengths and weaknesses. There is nothing prescriptive about the analysis; its purpose is to make areas of weakness and concern readily apparent.

In addition to the normal financial development analysis, in the context of an equity market development program, certain additional areas should be examined. These include the importance of public confidence, a profitable long-term outlook, some private ownership and free enterprise, political stability and support, and willingness to hold financial versus real assets.

Public Confidence

One of the major findings regarding equity markets in DCs is the extent of public confidence in the development of the financial system. No matter how well designed the institutions and how competent the regulation, financial system development can make little progress without public confidence. Moreover, while reforms are being implemented, every effort must be made to assure the public that the new policies are equitable, consistent, and rational and that they are designed to improve financial conditions in the country. Should public confidence be lacking, major government and private-sector efforts must be initiated to improve confidence in the system.

The caveat to public confidence in emerging domestic stock markets is that by definition these markets tend to be small and shallow. In that case asset price fluctuations are magnified, assets are less marketable therefore less liquid, and market efficiency is lacking. These conditions do not inspire public confidence. One way to counteract the damage is to make meticulous preparations before the stock market is established, including in-depth market research and a well-publicized campaign to educate the public about the benefits and risks of securities investments.

Long-term Outlook

Other conditions are also important during this analysis stage. Economic conditions must be viewed within the context of profitability of the private and state-owned enterprises (SOE). Firms must have a favorable long-term outlook if they are to be able to raise funds, either through loans, bonds, or equity. Without a favorable long-term outlook, investors will not be willing to invest funds unless they are assured of a rapid payback.

This long-term outlook is dependent also on the expectation of inflation. In the case of a mild inflationary environment equity securities have the potential to appreciate with inflation. This is an advantage over the erosion in value of debt instruments. However, the expectation of high inflation will inevitably drive investors to place their savings into real assets or stronger currencies outside the country. Consequently, it is of the utmost importance that inflation be contained in order to attract domestic savings.

Private Ownership and Free Markets

There must be some movement toward private ownership and allowing the market at least limited amounts of freedom. Equity markets cannot function to their fullest extent where central planning allocates goods to end users. This is not to say that total free markets and enterprise are necessary. The existence of the central planning mechanism in China, Hungary, and socialist countries, along with the growth of the equity markets in those countries, shows that, to a certain degree, they can exist in tandem. However coexistence is not enough. A free market economy offers something more: encouragement for free enterprises and private ownership to expand and prosper. This attitude on the part of the public and private sectors alike is an important element of equity market development.

Profits should be viewed as a positive and acceptable idea. The view that profits are unacceptable from an overall country perspective is not conducive to developing equity markets. Profits must be viewed as a reward for taking risk, and the differentiation of individuals by their ability to earn profits must be accepted.

Political Support and Stability

Political conditions need to be supportive of the development of an equity market. A major hindrance to the development of equity markets is the fact that governments, when equity markets are established, give up a considerable amount of control over the financial system (especially because most developing countries have bank-centered financial systems). Instead of direct control through credit regulations on financial institutions, there is indirect control of the monetary system through less powerful methods because companies can circumvent tight monetary policy by selling equity.

In addition, relatively stable political conditions should hold. In environments of instability, investors, if they invest at all, take a very short-term view, which causes a volatile market and is an anathema to any long-term planning by corporations. For example, in Argentina, companies obtain working capital by rolling over very short-term loans of seven days or less.

Financial versus Real Assets

To mobilize savings, they must be in financial asset form. The overall financial system does not benefit when investors put their money into real estate, gold, or other real assets. Real assets do not bring the benefits of financial assets because they cannot be loaned to other investors. Where inflation is excessive, this view is especially hard to develop. Indexed assets, although helpful as has been found in Chile and Brazil, are still insufficient to overcome the problems of high inflation.

Financial Development Strategy

The second major component of financial system development is the development of a medium- and long-term strategy of financial system reform in the light of broad national economic, social, and political objectives. This really entails two separate parts. The first is the understanding of broad government goals for the economy. This is important because the costs and benefits of a financial system development program can only be evaluated in the context of the overall goals of the economy. The second, based on those goals and objectives, is the development of a strategy of financial system reform. As with all development programs, these must be individual to each country. The blanket use of a single strategy for all countries may be ineffective as well as harmful to the development needs of the country.

In the context of an equity market development program, certain areas must be evaluated to ensure an adequate environment for the sale of shares. These include the official selling of the equity idea and the resolution of important questions regarding the financial system.

Official Selling of Equity Ideas

The official selling of equity ideas is a major challenge for many DCs. Many are unfamiliar with financial assets as a whole, and the concept of equity is relatively new. Moreover, in countries where inflation is relatively high, this further inhibits the development of equity as a viable alternative to real assets.

Selling the equity idea is a difficult political undertaking. Many long-standing ideas and concepts must be altered to accept equity as a viable investment alternative. In addition, long-standing concepts of individual and family ownership must also be changed as companies begin to issue shares.

One of the main challenges of developing countries is overcoming resistance to change. Often this is very difficult. In some countries, where resistance cannot be totally overcome, the main objective should be noninterference. An equity market can also be structured in different ways depending on the goals and objectives of each country. Because there is no "right" way to structure an equity market, the development of a market basically is eliminating as many obstacles as possible so that they will not impair the long-term development of the market.

Resolution of Important Questions

Next must be the resolution of important questions regarding financial markets in general and equity markets specifically. The answers to these questions must be based on the goals and objectives of the country.

What type of exchange? Should it be a private organization, or will the government have a direct participation? Generally most exchanges are private organizations (e.g., Singapore and Hong Kong). In other instances, the exchange is official in that the government owns the exchange but the members conduct business and regulate themselves. Generally, a private nonprofit corporation with shares owned by members is the recommended alternative.

What about government regulation? Should there be a single regulatory authority or several? Generally, a single regulatory authority has been recommended. In some countries, such as Turkey, there has been a tendency to require approval of both the regulatory authority and the Ministry of Finance regarding changes and regulatory activities. Because the regulatory authority, in most countries, is under the Ministry of Finance, this dual authority may be counterproductive.

What about market structure? Should transactions occur only on the exchange or should over-the-counter trading be allowed? In the initial stages of equity market development, there should be a single market with no over-the-counter trading allowed. The problems in the Indian market, with a large number of trades bypassing the market, have limited the depth of the market there.

What types of securities should be traded? Should options and futures be allowed? Again, both government securities and publicly listed companies should be allowed to trade shares, although, at least initially, options and futures should not be allowed. Later, as the market develops, additional instruments can be allowed.

Legislative and Policy Framework Design

The third component is the design of a legislative and policy framework, especially fiscal and monetary policy, conducive to the strategy and objectives of the country. Important in this area is the need to treat all instruments equally. Where instruments of equal risk are treated differently, a bias leading to an unfair advantage is created.

Equity market development should be a major portion of this component. It is not that equity instruments should have an advantage over other instruments. This is rarely the case. Usually equity instruments are treated differently than other similar instruments. Often, deposit interest is tax free whereas dividend income from equity investments is taxed. It should be a conscious policy objective not to discriminate against equity instruments. Because the development of an equity market has important benefits for the entire financial system, there should be a consensus that, for a period of time, equity market development is to be a major objective. During this period, equity markets and instruments will be given preferential treatment to stimulate development of the markets. The Capital Markets Law in Brazil in 1964 was a major stimulus to the development of the equity market, as has been the decision by the Korean government to promote actively the equity markets in the late 1970s.

Government Overview and Regulation

The fourth component is the construction of a system of governmental overview and regulation of financial institutions and markets in the interests of efficient intermediation and saver and investor protection. This is done best through a dialogue with the private sector. As with all other portions of financial system development, those government programs that have not included the private sector as important and necessary inputs to the development of the financial markets have been much more prone to failure than those where the private sector has taken an active role. Different institutions and markets require different regulatory frameworks. Moreover, often the best forms of regulation are a composite of private self-regulation with government oversight.

Within the context of equity market development, there must be the development of a regulatory agency to oversee the activities of the securities markets. Many countries, such as Korea and Turkey, have found that a self-regulatory institution working within the official regulatory system can be very beneficial both to the private business sector and the private investors. This agency is charged with the responsibility of serving the public by ensuring that markets operate in an orderly fashion and by enforcing laws and regulations for the public's protection.

Major purposes of government regulatory agencies in developing countries should include education to foster investor confidence, encouraging market growth, regulation, and institution building. Although regulation is important in the initial stages of equity market development, education, building investor confidence, and encouraging market growth should be the major objectives.

Supply of Trained Personnel

The fifth component is the provision of an adequate supply of trained personnel in both the public and private sectors to operate the financial system.

Many DCs are sending students abroad to study the necessary areas of finance, business, computers, and statistics to aid in the development of trained personnel. After their study, many are given positions in different types of financial institutions including investment banks, merchant banks, securities firms, brokers, and market makers, which will be valuable to the country when the students return. Moreover, international and central banks are important training grounds for personnel within the local environment. A supply of students studying and working in the investment banking and securities market firms is important for equity market development.

Public and Private Accounting and Auditing

Implementation of a satisfactory system of public and private accounting and auditing, together with rules on financial disclosure for public and private entities, is the next step. This is important to ensure that timely, accurate, and necessary information is available to the investing public, as well as to government regulatory bodies.

For investors to be willing to invest in equities, sufficient information must be available on which to base opinions about return and risk characteristics. For this reason, the periodic disclosure of relevant and accurate information is very important. In the securities field, a flow of relevant information is needed because the investor cannot, in effect, examine what he is buying, which is a call on the future earnings of the company.

Adequate and reliable financial information about issuers is fundamental to financial markets in general and to equity markets specifically. Companies must be required to maintain accurate books and records, financial statements should be audited by independent auditors, and financial statements should be prepared in compliance with rules established by the regulatory authority.

Development of Markets, Institutions, Services and Instruments

The final component for the development of a financial system is the development of an appropriate range of public and private financial instruments, as well as services, institutions, and markets. Different countries, in different stages of development, should phase the expansion of their financial systems with varying degrees of emphasis. Given the goals and objectives of the country and the current state of the financial system, it may be a suitable time to encourage an official equity market development program.

EQUITY MARKET DEVELOPMENT — A PROGRAM

With many types of operations it may be possible to perform activities sequentially, but with equity market development activities must be performed simultaneously. Many important areas need to be considered in light of a single program. Equity market development is not a simple process. Moreover, it is not a short-term activity to be turned on or off at will. Rather, it is a long-term commitment to a set of intermediary goals (called an equity market development program) that will aid the country in achieving its long-term goals and objectives.

Develop a Supply of Securities

Having enough stock to trade is often a major constraint for developing countries. Too few stocks with too few investors initially may keep investors from entering the market. Later, as the trading increases, too many investors bidding for too few stocks leads to price volatility and possibilities for a market crash.

The number of firms required to begin an equity market can be as few as 20, each with a float (the number of shares available to the public and outside institutional traders) of about 25 percent.[2] The stock markets of Korea, Jordan, and Thailand began with such relatively small numbers. Fiscal policies that may help increase the supply of shares are discussed in Chapter 5. Korea is an excellent example of a country that has actively sought to increase the supply of shares in the market.

Factors influencing the supply of securities include the size of the economy, its level of development, its free market orientation; the attitude of existing owners about allowing outsiders into the company and opening their books; the need for a sizable increase in funds, which often exceeds the ability of the owners to self-finance; the lack of the availability of low-cost and subsidy loans, which makes equity shares a viable alternative; pricing determined by market value, rather than government regulation pricing equities at their true worth; and the reduction in the amount of government ownership in firms by those shares being sold to the public.

Develop a Demand for Securities

At the same time, it is important to develop a demand for securities. A demand for securities comes from many areas: financially knowledgeable individuals with enough money to purchase shares; institutional demand from insurance companies, mutual funds, and pension funds that are not constrained by government regulation to invest only in government securities; and government controlled pension and social security funds that may invest in the equities market. In addition, foreign portfolio investment may also be an additional source of demand for equities.

Ideally, there should be minimal distortions from government influences from fiscal, monetary, and economic policies that influence both the supply and demand for securities. However, in the initial stages of market development these influences, if used correctly, may be very beneficial to the development of the market. Influences affecting the demand for shares are discussed in Chapter 6.

Fundamental Issues

As discussed earlier, many important questions must be answered before establishing an equity market. If the country waits until the last component of development to answer these important questions, much time will be lost. Ideally, these questions will be resolved during the initial stages of financial market development so that the private sector and government will be building the initial legal, institutional, and regulatory framework for development of the market. Items already discussed include a single exchange, no over-the-counter trades, initially no options and futures, a self-regulatory body to oversee the activities of exchange members, and a nonprofit exchange with shares held by various exchange members. In addition, to reduce volatility, there should initially be limited trading hours to give investors time to assimilate information, and trading should be limited to local investors only. As the market matures and develops, equity markets may be opened to nonresident citizens, then country funds, then perhaps convertible bonds, and finally full liberalization. India is an example of the successful mobilization of funds from nonresident Indians; Korea is an example of the successful use of country funds and convertible bonds.

Development of Self-Regulatory Agency

Development of the self-regulating agency should be encouraged at the same time that the exchange is established with adequate enforcement procedures. In addition, the government regulatory body should also be finalized, and both should work on education, institution building, regulation, and development of the market. The legal framework for establishing the exchange and the lines of authority of the government regulatory agency should also be clear.

Improvement of Financial Reporting

Initial reporting requirements for public firms may not be as detailed as is necessary. Work should continue on the development of detailed disclosure rules and the establishment of adequate auditing procedures to ensure timely, comparable, and accurate information to the investing public and regulatory agencies.

Institution Building and Training

Initially, training personnel will be an important challenge for the exchange members. Investment, merchant, and commercial banks may be an important source of trained personnel.

Importance of the Private Sector

Governments have the authority to require pension and other institutional investors to invest in government securities rather than in private equity. The government must not impose undue requirements on the percentage amount of government securities. The requirement that investors hold a large percentage of their assets in government securities has a direct negative effect on the development of the market.

CONCLUSION

Undoubtedly, the private sector must be the force that drives the financial system. Attempts by governments to control the marketplace have resulted in disastrous experiences. Nonetheless, governments must assume the important role of creating the appropriate environment to enable financial markets, especially equity markets, to develop freely. The preservation of this environment requires official regulation. A delicate balance of flexible regulations and private initiatives must be achieved. Thus regulations must be responsive to market conditions.

Future research is needed in the area of market liberalization, specifically equity markets. Empirical research into the stages of financial development of countries and its relationship to economic growth would be a useful endeavor. Another area of concern is the integration of emerging markets into world markets, its advantages and disadvantages as surmised from empirical research.

NOTES

1. This chapter was co-written with Dr. Marta Oyhenart of George Washington University as part of on-going research in sequencing in the equity market development process.

2. van Agtmael, *Emerging Securities Markets*, 45.

9

Case Studies

These case studies analyze three developing country equity markets within the environment in which they operate. However, because equity market development must be part of an overall financial system development program, many factors that cannot be covered in this book have an important effect on equity market development. These case studies cover the most important areas: historical financial framework, regulatory and institutional framework, primary and secondary markets, supply and demand for equities, institutional investors, internationalization of the markets, and a summary of major development patterns.

The historical financial framework section discusses briefly the important factors from the economic and political environment that have influenced the development of the equity market. The regulatory and institutional framework section discusses those environments in terms of the current equity market. The primary and secondary markets section briefly discusses the institutional structure of the countries regarding those markets. The supply and demand for equities section discusses interest rate policies and reasons underlying the lack of supply and demand for equities. The institutional investors section discusses the institutional policies relating to the market. And the internationalization of the equity market section discusses the foreign participation policies and opportunities for foreign portfolio investment. The final section, a summary of major development patterns, discusses the major factors that have had a major positive or negative effect on the development of the market in that country.

These case studies cover three countries, Brazil, India, and Korea, with each chosen for specific reasons. The basic outline for each case study is similar; the emphasis for each country differs because of differences in history, government, and cultural aspects.

BRAZIL

Brazil was chosen for five reasons: it has a large land mass and large population; it has very diverse peoples and cultures; it is geographically different from Korea and India; it has a functioning equity market that is relatively large by world standards; and in the mid-1960s it embarked on a program of major capital market development, which may be instructive to other DCs.

Historical Financial Framework

This section discusses the historical financial framework of Brazil. It covers three major stages: infant stage, rapid growth stage, and slow growth stage.

Infant Stage (1950–1963)

The Brazilian stock market dates from the mid-nineteenth century, when a group of brokers organized themselves on the model of the current French market. The market was characterized by trading in only a few stocks; bonds were completely unknown. There was little motivation for firms to go public because there was effectively no primary market. There was little motivation for individuals to invest. Companies' financial statements, if available, did not provide information necessary for investors. The lack of firms going public and the lack of company information, allied to the public's almost total ignorance of this kind of investment, relegated stock exchanges to an insignificant role in the financial system.

Interest rates in Brazil were constrained by a usury law to 12 percent. However, there were ways of circumventing this law, such as under-the-counter interest rates, accumulation of front-end fees, and "linked" bank accounts. These allowed banks to charge in excess of the legal ceiling. Virtually no financing other than lending by official institutions was available for investment in fixed assets.

High inflation, combined with the 12 percent ceiling on interest rates, led to a violent process of financial disintermediation. Demand deposits became the only financial asset of any importance within the sphere of responsibility of the financial system. The financial system itself was reduced to little more than the commercial banks.[1] These factors and others contributed to the reasons for the financial system reform of 1964.

Rapid Growth Stage (1964–1976)

Financial system reform during 1964 was shaped by three key laws: the Banking Reform Law, the Housing Finance Law, and the Capital Markets Law. These laws made monetary policy the responsibility of the newly created National Monetary Council (CMN), created a Central Bank, and established the Housing Finance System headed by the National Housing Bank (BNH). Monetary authority was divided between the Central Bank and the Bank of Brazil, with their combined responsibilities going far beyond conventional central banking. To encourage financial savings, a range of assets bearing monetary correction (indexation of the principal) was introduced. Fiscal incentives were also provided to promote manufactured exports, to aid the formation of risk capital, and to strengthen the equity market.

The financial system following the reforms differed from a unified financial market. The most striking features were market segmentation and the proliferation of selective credit programs; few loan rates set by market conditions; the existence of assets with and without monetary correction; key role of state financial intermediation; increasing conglomeration of the private financial sector; and the mixed banking role assumed by the Monetary Authorities and the consequent use of quantitative targets specified in an annual monetary budget to control lending levels directly.

During this period, the government realized the importance of the capital markets as means of harnessing domestic resources. Legislation regarding the equity market in Brazil had begun in 1964 with Law 4506 and Open Capital Stock Companies, and was further developed with the Capital Markets Law of 1965.

Law 4506 addressed the development of the equity market by using fiscal treatment to increase supply. It created the concept of Open Capital Stock Companies (SACA) with preferential fiscal treatment. Open capital companies are those with shares traded on the exchanges, with a minimum of 30 percent of the firm's voting rights owned by more than 200 stockholders, with each one owning no more than 3 percent of total shares.

Major innovations from the Capital Markets Law included mandatory registration of securities issued and traded through the securities distribution system; transformation of Public Funds Brokers through whom all stock exchange operations were channeled into individual firms or brokerage houses; establishment of a constitution for the stock exchange, including definitions of modus operandi and functions of the exchanges; creation of investment banks; creation of tax incentives for companies to list their capital; and creation of tax incentives for individuals and corporations to invest in securities.

In an attempt to finance the working capital needs of open capital companies, to develop the capital markets, and to educate the public regarding the benefits of investing, Decree Law 157 was passed creating fiscal investment funds. This law allowed investors to deduct a portion of their income tax due the government and use it for the purchase of stock certificates through financial institutions. These institutions formed investment funds and invested the proceeds in shares and debentures that could not be withdrawn by the investor for five and a half years.

These "157 Funds" were an immediate success. Amounts invested in shares and debenture increased form Cs$18 billion in 1978 to Cs$1,712 billion in 1984. Giving up current revenue for the development of long-term capital was an important step for the government and a large boost to the development of the capital markets in Brazil. However, demand soon exceeded supply. Prices rose quickly, as too many funds were chasing too few outstanding shares. Share prices rose dramatically, with a major correction coming in late 1971 resulting in the "crisis of 1971." This crash was a major setback in the market and resulted in many firms not coming to the market to raise funds for a long time. It also reinforced to many individuals the value of real estate as the best investment hedge.

Slow Growth Stage (1972–1985)

The slow growth stage was very turbulent for business and industry. In an effort to improve reporting and earlier tax collection, the government enacted additional legislation concerned with the quality of information available to the public. In addition to its aid to government, an important side effect was its aid to the development of the equity market because it increased the amount of information to the investing public.

Government policy in Brazil favored credit subsidies. However, these subsidies and financial fragmentation became a major source of inflationary pressure, policy-induced distortions, and allocative efficiency losses. By 1979, annual interest rate differentials between different segments of the credit market reached over 70 percent. The difficulty of controlling so many highly selective credit lines is responsible for many of the problems encountered in containing levels of economic activity and inflation after 1974.

The levels of credit subsidies do not appear to have been consciously planned. The policy of maintaining an overvalued exchange rate and compensating adversely affected sectors by credit and fiscal subsidies imposed a massive resource drain on the public sector because of the use of quantitative restrictions on imports and prohibitively high tariffs. However, tariff receipts totaled only 7 percent of Treasury Receipts in 1978; Monetary Authorities and fiscal incentives to manufactured exports totaled 49 percent.

In 1976, Law 6404, the New Corporation law, introduced new legislation governing publicly quoted corporations. It set the target of creating an institutional framework that would facilitate the development of the stock market, including standardization of financial statements, disclosure policy, treatment of minority holders of voting stock, and regulation of debentures.

Along this same line, Law 5589 of 1970 was passed requiring companies with traded stock to submit biannual reports to the exchanges. Other resolutions, seeking improved accounting practices and disclosure of financial information, followed.

Brazil's economic condition continued to deteriorate. Worsening of the international environment was marked by a near halving of the terms of trade over 1977–1982, higher nominal and real interest charges and spreads, and a partial withdrawal of foreign lenders. By mid-1983 Brazil had experienced two and a half years of negative per capita growth. National savings had declined from 20.8 percent in 1977 to 15.9 percent in 1981. Inflation continued in the triple digits amid uncertainty caused by general changes in government policy.

Credit subsidies increased sharply with rising inflation as it had previously, but by 1980 Brazil had reached the unstable point where higher inflation was associated with a lower inflation tax yield. In 1981, massive internal borrowing was initiated, and attempts were made to shift the subsidy burden to the commercial banks. But the bank's access to low-cost demand deposits was shrinking rapidly.

Quantitative limits on domestic lending grew tighter. Public debt absorbed surplus funds, which could not otherwise be lent domestically because of quantitative limits. Real credit volumes were halved between 1980 and 1981. These limits forced borrowers to turn abroad for funds.

Large spreads developed between domestic loan and deposit rates after the former were freed in November 1980. Even prime borrowers paid 40 percent to 50 percent per annum in real terms for funds.

Inflation continued to rise from 1983 to 1987. Inflation, as measured by the Brazilian CPI was 142 percent in 1983, 197 percent in 1984, 227 percent in 1985, 145 percent in 1986, and 312 percent in the first nine months of 1987.

In 1986, the government attempted to introduce a wage-price freeze under the Cruzado Plan. It was an attempt to break the circle of high inflation, weak currency, and high real interest rates. After initial optimism, the plan soon began to crumble and the government was forced to introduce selective price increases. By November 1986 inflation was 3 percent per month, which increased to 17 percent per month in February 1987.

At that time the government declared a debt moratorium, suspending interest payments on its international debt. After a short period of reassessment, Brazil has followed a policy of major objectives, including to reach rescheduling agreements with banks, convert some of the debt into equity, stimulate new foreign investment, increase the trade surplus, control government deficits, and de-index the economy to attempt to reduce inflation.

The current situation in Brazil remains uncertain. It is very difficult for any country's economy to experience significant real growth with such a high rate of inflation.

Major themes during the past two decades have included inflation, financial segmentation, and credit subsidies; all are highly intertwined. Instead of cutting government expenditures in Brazil (politically a very unpopular activity), spending and credit subsidies have increased. These have led, as expected, to an increase in inflation. While the public sector is nearly bankrupt, however, the private sector has been recording vigorous and solid development. Balance sheets have little debt, and Brazilian firms are developing a worldwide reputation for quality products at reasonable prices. However, the deficit impedes public-sector investment in infrastructure and expends the scant national savings in an unproductive fashion, to the detriment of the private sector. At the same time, the deficit excites financial market instability because of the alarmist visions of the impossibility of maintaining the debt-financing process. Clearly, important actions need to be taken.

Regulatory and Institutional Framework

Regulatory Framework

The regulatory framework in Brazil is composed of institutions with the classic policy-making functions: the National Monetary Council (Conselho Monetario Nacionao), the Central Bank (Banco Central do Brasil), and the Securities Commission (Comissao de Valores Mobiliarios). It also includes institutions charged with implementing specific government programs: the Bank of Brazil (Banco de Brasil), the BNDES (Banco Nacional de Desenvolvimento Economico e Social), and the National Housing Bank (Banco Nacional da Habitacao).

Major enabling legislation for the regulatory framework was Law 4380 of 1964 creating the Housing Finance System; Law 4595 of 1964, the Banking Reform Law, creating the National Monetary Council and regulating monetary, banking, and credit institutions; and Law 6385 of 1976 creating the "Comissao de Valores Mobiliarios" (Brazilian Securities Commission). These three laws were designed to create a segmented financial system in which some institutions would become the sole suppliers of credit to certain sectors of the economy. This attempt to divide the market between the operation of the credit market and intermediation in securities could not achieve clear differentiation because of the establishment of financial conglomerates, which included institutions operating in every segment of the financial system. The conglomerates were under the leadership of commercial banks.

The National Monetary Council, as established by the Banking Reform Law, is the highest level normative body and is integrated by state ministers, presidents, and directors of the main financial institutions of the system, as well as representatives of private entities. It formulates exchange and monetary policies, coordinates credit, budget, fiscal, internal and external debt policies, and regulates the creation, operations, and surveillance of financial institutions.

The Central Bank, also established under the Banking Reform Law, is responsible for the control and execution of monetary policy. It issues money, receives reserve deposits of financial institutions, controls credit, oversees open-market operations, controls foreign capital, and holds foreign exchange deposits.

Although the Banking Law appeared to pave the way toward a more orthodox monetary authority, its institutional changes were more cosmetic than substantive. The relative autonomy and the limits of action of the Central Bank and the 75 percent state-owned Bank of Brazil are still not clearly defined.

The Bank of Brazil is a public company whose major shareholder is the federal government. It is the main governmental institution operating credit and financial policies. It performs the double role of monetary authority and commercial bank, sharing monetary authority and holding voluntary reserves of the commercial banking system. It is a financial agent of the Treasury, executes clearing functions, makes foreign exchange transactions, executes foreign trade policy, and extends special credit.

The Securities Commission, established by law 6385, is responsible for registering and supervising public companies, public issues, independent auditors, and securities analysts. It supervises the issuance and distribution of securities, trading and intermediation in securities, stock exchange trading, administration of securities markets, auditing of public companies, the services of consultants and analysts, and the disclosure of information to the market.

Institutional Framework

The institutional framework in Brazil is composed of both private and public financial institutions. These institutions operate with different types of financial assets. Those institutions operating with fixed income securities include commercial banks, federal and state savings banks, investment banks, and other financial institutions. Those institutions operating with risky securities (specifically equities) include stock exchanges, brokerage firms, distribuidoras, mutual and fiscal funds, foreign capital investments companies, and investment companies.

Brazil's financial system is specialized by law. However, banking conglomerates tend to own brokerage houses and distributors, as well as investment banks, finance companies, and housing credit institutions. As a result, Brazil's banking conglomerates often represent multibanks, banks which not only perform regular banking functions but also act as broker/dealers and institutional investors in the securities markets.

Fixed Income Securities. Commercial banks are basically concentrated on short- and medium-term loans. They accept demand and time deposits extending credit to firms and to the public. In March 1985 the top ten commercial banks held 74 percent of demand deposits and 52 percent of time deposits.

Federal and State Savings Banks are members of the Housing Finance System. They operate housing and mortgage loans and receive time and savings deposits. They are not active in demand deposits but hold more than half as savings deposits.

Investment banks are mainly involved in acquisitions and medium- and long-term financing. They operate mainly with their own risk capital and funds raised through time deposits. In March 1985 they held about 36 percent of total time deposits.

State and regional development banks provide long- and medium-term financing in their respective region or state. Savings and loan associations and cooperatives provide housing finance. Finance companies issue acceptance letters to finance durable goods whereas leasing companies operate in real estate and in leasing durable goods.

Risky Securities. Stock exchanges are nonprofit private associations designed to provide an adequate place for trading stocks and other financial assets. The largest exchanges are in Rio de Janeiro and Sao Paulo.

Brokerages' firms are members of the stock exchange in which they operate. They buy, sell, and distribute securities on their own and for the public and may coordinate public offerings. In addition, they provide portfolio, fund, and investment club management, as well as transacting in the open market.

Distribuidoras engage in open-market transactions and can sell securities to the public and buy and sell for their own account. They can also subscribe issues for resale or intermediate the issues in the market. They cannot buy and sell on the stock exchanges as they are not members of the exchange.

Mutual and fiscal funds are not financial institutions but operate under the surveillance of the Central Bank. The funds raised are invested in stocks, debentures, and fixed income assets. They are managed by investment banks, brokerage firms, and distribuidoras.

Foreign capital investment companies are companies with capital subscribed by foreign firms and individuals for investment in Brazilian securities. Their portfolios must be managed by licensed brokerage firms or investment banks.

Primary and Secondary Equity Markets

The development of the equity market of Brazil had most of its beginnings with the financial reforms of 1964. Periods of high inflation during the late 1950s and 1960s had strong disintermediation effects. The Castelo Branco government, in a far-sighted move, instituted major reforms to support resumption of economic growth and stability, including capital market reforms as part of an overall financial system development program. However later governments, in attempts to increase short-term government revenues and obtain lower-than-market rate funds, have passed legislation that has seriously affected equity market development. This section discusses primary markets and secondary markets. Statistics regarding the primary and secondary equity market in Brazil are found in Table 9.1 and Figure 9.1.

Primary Markets

New issues of equity securities by business firms in Brazil are currently controlled by the Brazilian Securities Commission. Primary markets are concerned mainly with new offerings of stock of open-capital companies on the exchanges. In Brazil there are two major exchanges and eight other smaller exchanges.

Although more developed than in many countries, equity markets have not been a major source of funds for companies in Brazil. Major sources of funds include direct government investment, subsidized credit, retained earnings, and savings of family groups. Initial public offerings have been decreasing since 1982. About US$520 million was raised in new capital by 40 companies in 1985.

One method of encouraging supply is through subsidized credit. Subsidized credit is provided through two programs of the BNDE system, PROCAP and FINAC. These programs encourage underwriting and equity purchases by individuals in open-capital companies, while BNDE subsidiaries support equity through the direct purchases of preferred, nonvoting stock in Brazilian enterprises.

Secondary Markets

There are ten active stock exchanges in Brazil; the Rio de Janeiro and the Sao Paulo Stock Exchanges are the largest and represent about 95 percent of total transactions. Listings on the Sao Paulo exchange have increased from 404 in 1979 to 590 in 1987. Listings on the Rio de Janeiro exchange have increased from 574 in 1976 to 650 in 1987.

Market capitalization in Brazil (market price per share times the number of shares outstanding) has increased from US$17.2 billion in 1977 to US$16.9 billion in 1987. Trading volume has also increased. Volume on the exchanges has increased from US$2.6 billion in 1976 to US$9.6 billion in 1987. As measures of performance in dollar terms, the Emerging Markets Database index of the International Finance

TABLE 9.1
Brazil Market Statistics — Currency Amounts in Millions

	1985	1986	1987 Q1	1987 Q2	1987 Q3	1987 Q4	1988 Q1	1988 Q2	1988 Q3
A. NUMBER OF LISTED COMPANIES									
1) Sao Paulo Bolsa de Valores	541	592	594	592	596	590	585	580	587
2) Rio de Janeiro Bolsa de Valores	615	658	-	-	-	-	650	636	630
B. MARKET CAPITALIZATION									
1) In Cruzados (Sao Paulo only)	448,641	612,327	438,775	902,190	1,200,758	1,202,942	2,908,960	5,164,507	10,911,378
2) In US Dollars	42,768	42,096	19,815	20,799	23,415	16,900	25,177	26,535	30,211
C. TRADING VALUE									
Rio de Janeiro Bolsa de Valores	65,951	150,461	17,396	39,067	51,213	36,134	100,093	370,241	426,400
Sao Paulo Bolsa de Valores	67,262	244,298	23,369	47,625	68,799	93,311	225,524	466,597	511,671
1) Total in Cruzados	133,213	394,759	40,765	86,692	120,012	129,446	325,617	836,838	938,071
2) In US Dollars	21,485	28,912	2,230	2,530	2,537	2,155	3,544	5,487	3,488
3) Turnover Ratio	29.7	64.5	9.3	9.6	10.0	10.8	11.2	16.2	8.6
D. LOCAL INDEX									
1) BOVESPA Market Index (1968=0.1)*	655.4	925.8	663.4	1,112.6	1,480.8	1,248.6	3,964.8	7,037.2	13,692.0
2) Change in Index (%)	401.5	41.3	-28.3	67.7	33.1	-15.7	217.5	77.5	94.6
E. EMERGING MARKETS DATA BASE									
1) Number of Stocks in EMDB Sample	26	29	30	30	30	30	30	30	30
2) EMDB Share of Market Cap. (%)	27.4	28.9	33.1	27.8	25.8	26.0	30.1	31.4	26.0
3) EMDB Total Returns Index(Dec/84=100)	195.0	148.0	78.4	71.8	75.7	54.8	99.3	110.1	108.4
4) Change in EMDB Index(%)	95.0	-24.1	-47.0	-8.5	5.6	-27.6	81.2	10.8	-1.5
F. EXCHANGE RATES									
1) Exchange Rates (End of Period)	10.4900	14.5460	22.1440	43.3760	51.2820	71.1800	115.5400	194.6300	361.1700
2) Exchange Rates (Average of Period)	6.2004	13.6540	18.2800	34.2687	47.3100	60.0590	91.8780	152.5121	268.9543

*The BOVESPA Index was divided by 10 at August 29, 1988. The series reflects this division.

Source: Quarterly Review, 38.

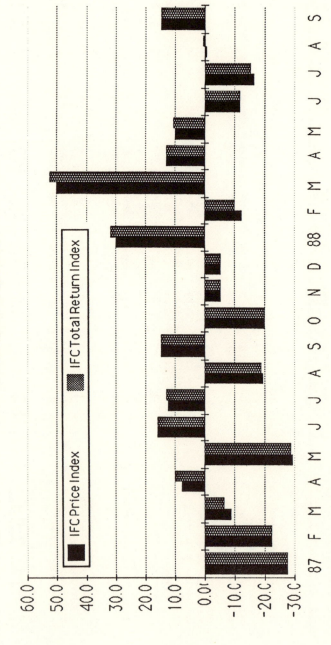

Monthly Performance Since January 1987
Monthly % Change in US$

IFC Price Index
IFC Total Return Index

FIGURE 9.1 — Brazil
Source: Quarterly Review, 39.

Corporation increased from 100 in December 1975 (base year) to 78 in 1987. The index calculated by the Sao Paulo Stock Exchange in Brazilian currency increased from 1.93 in December 1975 (January 2, 168 = 1) to 19,089 in January 1988. However, because of currency appreciation, on a dollar basis, setting December 1975 as 100, the market would have decreased to 71. However, in the first 10 months of 1988, the market increased by 128 percent in dollar terms.

Brazil's secondary markets experienced a boom in 1985 and 1988. Records were set in trading volume and price rises. One occurrence of note was the sale of shares in Petrobras, the national oil company. Over US$500 million was raised as part of the government's privatization program. The Petrobras offer brought 300,000 new investors to the market, virtually doubling the shareholder base in Brazil. It is hoped that other similar offerings will occur.

Because of the large role played by retained profits, many sectors are still substantially closed. Many of the major Brazilian companies do not issue shares for public acquisition, and majority shareholders, often representatives of traditional family interests, hold about two-thirds of the equity of open-capital firms.

The Brazilian Equity Market also has a high percentage of government and state-owned enterprises. Of the largest open Brazilian enterprises, the government has substantial equity positions, which in 1977 accounted for 61 percent of total market capitalization. Although this has decreased since 1977, the government still controls major blocks of open companies.

Probably for this reason minority equity investment by individuals tends to concentrate on public-sector enterprises whereas equity funds and other official lending go to private nonfinancial Brazilian firms.

Factors other than stock market structure and subsidized credit contribute to the failure of the equity market to mobilize a greater portion of gross domestic financial savings for share purchases. A major factor is the availability of less risky, liquid indexed financial assets, with almost guaranteed return, and the attractiveness of financing current and capital expenditures through credit provided at subsidized, frequently negative, real rates through the BNDE system.

Supply and Demand for Equity

Supply of Shares

Many reasons explain the lack of supply of equity in Brazil. One of the reasons is the fear of loss of control. Another is that benefits from going public are not sufficient to compensate for the costs of additional disclosure requirements, greater public scrutiny, and fewer opportunities for tax evasion. Also, with budgetary pressures increasing, there are few government incentives to go public.

Demand for Shares

One of the major reasons for the lack of demand for share is the lack of adequate returns. With inflation at such high levels, returns have not been adequate to compensate for the higher risk in real terms. Inflation has reinforced the traditional notion that real estate and other real assets are the best types of inflation hedges. And, with indexed assets giving higher guaranteed returns, equity is not as attractive as other alternatives. In addition, demand incentives have been reduced to the point there are few incentives to invest in shares.

Institutional Investors

One of the major forces aiding equity market development in developing countries has been the growth of institutional investors. These have helped support the demand for shares in addition to other important factors. The institutional market in Brazil is one of the most advanced of all the developing countries. Institutional investors in Brazil include fiscal investment funds, mutual funds, investment clubs, investment companies (Decree Law 1401 companies), private pension funds, and insurance companies' and social participation funds. Brazilian 1401 Investment Companies and Fiscal Funds have over 90 percent of their assets in shares and debentures; Mutual Funds have about one-half of their assets in shares and debentures; and Pension Funds have only about one-quarter of their assets in shares and debentures.

Fiscal Investment Funds

One of the major strategies for the development of the primary and secondary market was Decree Law 157. Fiscal Investment Funds, or 157 Funds, were created to finance the working capital of open companies, develop capital markets, and educate the individual investor. Investors could, until 1983, deduct a portion of the income tax due and use it for the purchase of stock certificates through financial institutions. These institutions formed investment funds and invested the proceeds in shares and debentures. Redemptions by the investor were not permitted for five and a half years.

The 157 Funds have always had the most restrictive regulation, mostly favoring Brazilian companies in the private sector. In 1972, 25 percent of the portfolio value had to be invested in small and medium-sized companies; a maximum of 25 percent could be in the purchase of shares on the Stock Exchanges; and the remaining balance was invested in shares or companies controlled by private Brazilian open-capital corporations. Criteria for diversification were identical to those applied to mutual funds: a maximum of 10 percent could be invested in the shares of any one company, the average investments per company could not exceed 5 percent of the value of the funds portfolio, and the investment per company could not exceed 20 percent of the total capital.

In the years that followed, the rules governing 157 Funds changed several times until, in 1978, the investment per company was restricted to 4 percent of the capital, and the investment was limited to a maximum of 10 percent of the voting capital of a given company. Besides this, the total value of the portfolio to be invested in shares or debentures convertible into shares of Brazilian companies in the private sector was increased to 80 percent.

From 1980 on, the government, in an effort to cut subsidies (rather than part of a conscious plan), began gradually reducing the percentage of tax deductions, finally eliminating the tax benefit in 1983. Although there is still discussion regarding the costs of Law 157, Fiscal Investment Funds were very effective in stimulating equity market development.

Mutual Funds

The first mutual funds in Brazil appeared in the late 1950s and developed quickly until 1973. As in the 157 Funds case, the rules on composition of mutual funds underwent successive changes. Initially, Central Bank Resolution 145 of 1970 required mutual funds to keep 60 percent of their portfolios invested in shares and convertible debentures. Diversification standards were the same as for 157 Funds. Resolution 145 was rewritten in 1975 as Resolution 327, which, in addition to the 60 percent requirement, established as a diversification standard that no more than 10 percent of the total portfolio could be invested in securities issued by a single company and that no more than 10 percent of a company's voting stock or 20 percent of a company's total equity could be held by a single mutual fund. In addition, average holdings in a single company's securities might not exceed 5 percent of the overall portfolio.

Since the end of 1982, rising expectations about greater flexibility by mutual funds led to a rise in the number of participants. However, Central Bank Resolution 817, although it allowed freely organized portfolios, did not allow mutual funds to adapt to the new rules, which would have made it possible for money market funds, successful in the United States, to come to Brazil.

Law 4728 helped investments in mutual funds by granting a 15 percent tax incentive. Then in 1974, Law 1338 changed the deduction from income tax payable to only 9 percent of amounts invested in mutual funds. In 1976, this figure was increased to 13.5 percent. The tax incentive was eliminated in 1980.

In 1983, Decree Law 2072 allowed the government to charge income tax on the revenue earned by mutual funds on debentures in their portfolios. Moreover, National Monetary Resolution 961 introduced important changes in the allowable investments of mutual funds. Funds were classified as either fixed-income or variable-income funds, with the requirement that 60 percent of fixed-income funds and 30 percent of variable-income funds be invested in government securities.

The combination of these last two measures had a negative effect both on the industry and the market as a whole. With the imposition of these laws, the profit potential of the funds, especially fixed-income funds, was greatly reduced. Other types of instruments became more attractive to investors. In addition, having to pay income taxes to which they had been exempt further depressed profit potential.

These measures were very detrimental to the development of the equity and debenture markets. With the inclusion of the 60 percent and 30 percent requirements, resources available for the primary and secondary markets, after investing in government securities, were reduced considerably.

Investment Clubs

One of the results of a group established by the Securities Commission to aid in the development of the market (CODIMEC) was the creation of investment clubs. They were established because many thought that existing mechanisms, such as mutual funds, did not offer a significantly intense form of participation to start operating in the market and thus acquire experience and a working knowledge of the securities business. The Securities Commission issued Instruction 40, which defined the nature of the investment clubs and established general operating rules, restricting business in speculative markets, requiring registration on stock exchanges, and limiting the number of participants to 50. Tax treatment was defined by the Federal Revenue Secretariat in Regulatory Instruction #111, which classified the clubs as individuals, subject only to income tax at source on the revenue they obtained from securities. Investment clubs increased dramatically in the succeeding months.

Foreign Investment Companies (Decree Law 1401 Companies)

The investment of foreign resources in the stock market was permitted in 1975, under Decree Law 1401. Law 1401 established special investment companies that obtained resources abroad by selling their own stock and used those resources for the purchase of shares and debentures on the stock market.

Investments were regulated regarding the composition and diversification of the portfolios. At least 50 percent of the portfolio had to be invested in shares and convertible debentures of open companies, controlled by private Brazilian capital, acquired by subscription or on the trading floor of the stock exchanges. Limits were set on participation in voting capital and total capital per company, as well as on portfolio risk reduction and diversification.

Taxes and redemption period, which were the main reason for their poor performance when originally established, were later modified by Decree Law 1986 of 1982 and Central Bank Resolution 790 of 1983. Redemption, which was permitted in 20 percent portions of invested capital per year starting from the third year after entry of resources, fell to three months. Income tax, which was 15 percent of capital gains and dividends, was reduced to 15 percent of dividends only.

As a result of high taxes, long redemption periods (although later modified), and the difficulties that the Brazilian economy has been facing in recent years, the system established under Decree Law 1401 has largely collapsed.

Private Pension Funds

Investments by the private pension funds have been increasing greatly during the past four years. Pension funds in shares and debentures represent almost half of the total of the institutional investors. This portion indicates the importance of this segment to the development of the primary market and to the liquidity of the secondary market. Equally important, at medium term the growth rate of the equity of these institutions tends to remain steady. This situation may be expected to ensure a regular flow of resources to the market.

Original National Monetary Council regulations of 1977 required pension funds to invest between 20 percent and 40 percent of their stockholders' equity in shares and convertible debentures, with an additional 30 percent in government securities. In 1983, the 40 percent ceiling was eliminated, and the requirement of investing in government securities was reduced to 20 percent.

However, the trend toward free investments halted in 1984 with Resolutions 963 and 964 of the National Monetary Council. These required 45 percent of the resources of closed and open social security institutions be invested in government securities. In addition, investments by montepios and foundations in shares and debentures were limited to 20 percent. Besides withdrawing resources from the market, these actions made the investment profile very rigid, further hindering the market's development.

Insurance Companies and the Social Participation Fund

Insurance companies are beginning to develop in Brazil. Insurance companies are required to hold technical reserves and to invest between 30 percent and 45 percent in the form of shares and debentures, with half of this amount invested in securities of private Brazilian companies in the private sector. There were 96 insurance companies in Brazil in 1984.

The Social Participation Fund (PIS/PASEP) established in 1977, had no clearly defined commitment to the securities market but has channeled growing volumes of funds into the equity market. In 1982 they channeled Cr$21.5 billion into equities, Cr$132.5 billion in 1983, ad Cr$361.8 billion in the first nine months of 1984.

The institutional market is developing in Brazil, although recent government actions have limited its progress. Institutional investors have played an important part in Brazilian equity market development. For example, they have supplied a consistent demand for securities, improved liquidity in the markets, helped in encouraging improved reporting standards, brought in limited amounts of foreign capital, and helped educate investors about the opportunities and risks of the securities market.

Internationalization of the Equity Market

Brazil, like many developing countries, faces two basic constraints: the domestic savings gap and the external resource gap. Both gaps are critically important to transforming an economy from a simple structure in which primary production and primary products dominate, to a more complex structure in which manufacturing has a higher share in total output, industrial production a greater share of exports, and unemployed or underemployed resources drawn to higher levels of production and employment. In an effort to fill the external resource gap, Brazil has attempted internationalization of the equity market. Brazil was the first country, with a nonconvertible currency, to actively seek foreign investment. This was done through so-called 1401 Funds.

Decree Law 1401 of 1975 and Central Bank Resolution 323 were the enabling acts for the entry of foreign capital. These laws authorized the formation of investment companies or societies, giving favorable treatment to funds held for longer periods of time. Repatriation of capital was allowed only on a percentage of the original investment, with tax treatment dependent on the amount of original investment repatriated.

The most well-known of these funds was probably the Brazil Fund, S.A., sponsored by F&C Management, Ltd., Murry Johnstone, Ltd., Touche, Remnant & Co., and Vickers, da Costa & Co. From an initial investment of US$14.3 million, the return has been substantially negative. Although the initial idea was good, taxation and repatriation conditions did not attract the foreign capital that was expected. The popularity of 1401 Funds, which never exceeded US$60 million, was short-lived because of the poor performance of the market and the severe restrictions imposed on the funds. Later changes to the tax rates and repatriation of funds in 1983 eased the severity of the regulations, but because of the economic conditions at the time, entry of new capital to the Brazilian market was very limited.

Decree Law 1986 of 1982 was a response to the complaints of the 1401 Fund investors. The onerous three-year requirement was trimmed to three months, and the capital-gains tax was eliminated.

The most recent relation of Decree 2285, passed in July 1986, eliminated the tax on dividends and extended the exemption to mutual investment funds, as well as to investment companies. The decree covers funds registered with the Brazilian SEC. This allows foreign management of portfolios whereas before investors had to defer to Brazilian managers.

No Brazilian companies have yet been permitted to issue American Depositary Receipts (ADRs), nor have there been any convertible Eurobond issues. Although this would be very desirable for Brazil to gain exposure, the government is relinquishing control only gradually.

As of 1988, there has been little public discussion of a long-term plan for internationalization of the Brazilian securities market. However, with the external resource gap still growing, the need to attract foreign funds is becoming increasingly important. The government of Brazil is believed to be seriously considering improving access to the securities markets for foreign portfolio investment.

Major Development Patterns

Although Brazil had an early equity market development program in the early 1960s, it did not continue the program through the 1970s and 1980s. However, much of the depth of the market today is directly attributed to early market development efforts. This next section discusses the major development patterns that have had both a positive and a negative effect on the development of the equity market in Brazil.

Positive Development Factors

157 Funds/Fiscal Incentives. One of the major drivers of the development of the equity market was the development of the 157 Funds. This method was a government choice to channel tax revenues to the stock market to achieve three major objectives: to provide share capital for small and medium-sized Brazilian firms; to attract and educate individual investors about the stock markets, and to strengthen the stock markets by providing a steady source of support. This method of encouraging demand for securities had a great positive influence on the development of the equity market and achieved, to a great degree, each of the objectives. Although the positives have been emphasized, excess demand was a major reason for the market correction of 1971. Equity market development requires a balanced program of supply and demand.

Investment Clubs. Investment clubs, although without much history regarding their performance, seem to be a good method for encouraging individuals to learn about the market. From tentative indications, there is a great interest in individuals making their own decisions regarding the investment of their funds. As education regarding the stock market increases, greater numbers of investors should theoretically desire to channel their own investments through this type of club.

Requirements to Invest in Securities. Brazil has done well in developing private-sector pension and insurance systems and in requiring these institutional investors to invest in securities and convertible debentures. The additional funds brought to the market by institutional investors has greatly expanded the primary market and encouraged liquidity on the secondary market, making the market more attractive to borrowers and investors alike.

Progressive Elimination of Investment Incentives. Establishing fiscal incentives when a market is beginning to grow and gradually eliminating them as the market matures is an important concept for Brazil and other developing countries. However, the elimination of incentives in Brazil's case appears to be more a response to economic conditions than a gradual elimination of incentives as the market has developed. Of more benefit would have been publicizing the timetable for the gradual reduction of the incentives when the incentives were initiated, giving greater planning abilities to the investment community.

Government Privatization Efforts. With the sale of Petrobras, the national oil company, over US$500 million was raised and 300,000 new investors were brought to the equity market. This is an important first step in moving the economy toward a position necessary for greater long-term growth.

Conscious Designation of a Central Market Authority. Brazil made the decision to have all securities market institutions under a single central market authority. This has allowed consistency across exchanges and helped instill greater confidence in market operations.

Negative Development Factors

Requirements for Investment. With Resolution 961, the National Monetary Authority required mutual funds to invest 60 percent and 30 percent of their investments, depending on type of funds, in government securities. This lowered the profitability of the funds, causing investors to shift to other alternatives.

The requirements that institutional investors hold a certain percentage of their funds in government securities beyond prudent limits is a hindrance to equity market development. As the percentages increase, the number of resources available to the market is limited, contracting the market.

Investors not willingly investing in government securities should indicate that the securities are not correctly priced, given the limited risk that should prevail on government securities and other available alternatives.

Currently, the choice of investments by PIS/PASEP funds is at the discretion of the government. Allowing PIS/PASEP funds to seek the highest prudently diversified return would stimulate greater competition and therefore greater efficiency in the marketplace. The major problem seems to be whether these funds are viewed as property of the government or property of the investors.

Abrupt Changes in Government Policy. Planning for investment purposes requires estimates about future real returns. Although conditions arise that often require reevaluation of policy, abrupt changes to meet short-term goals do not inspire the confidence necessary for equity market development. To again achieve confidence in the financial system, confidence must be restored by long-term planning and follow-through.

Administered Credit Lines. Subsidized credit lines have been a great hindrance to equity market development in Brazil. Phasing out the extensive and complex system of administered credit lines at subsidized rates would permit the financial system to assume its proper intermediation role, with responsibility for mobilizing and allocating resources, relying on market mechanisms.

In addition, the levels of credit subsidies in Brazil do not appear to have been consciously planned. The policy of maintaining an overvalued exchange rate and compensating adversely affected sectors by credit and fiscal subsidies imposed a massive resource drain on the public sector because of the use of quantitative restrictions on imports and prohibitively high tariffs.

The government's channeling credit toward real estate, housing, and related investments has also hindered equity market development. This action appears to have contributed to considerable increases in land and property values, confirming the traditional view of real estate as the most successful hedge against inflation. The Brazilian market appears to be a victim of the segmented structure of the Brazilian financial market, which, by diverting funds toward alternative assets and substituting subsidized state funds for industrial borrowing on a free capital market, has rendered a savings-deficit sector and so inhibited the market's development.

Moreover, redistributing potential surpluses to the private sector as selective fiscal incentives rather than as reductions in tax rates does not appear to achieve the maximum benefit possible. This is partially due to many firms not taking advantage of the fiscal incentives available.

Segmentation of the Financial System. Because of the selective administration of credit, there is a great segmentation between official financial institutions, and the private financial institutions continue to operate under serious constraints. The supply of credit from commercial and state controlled financial institutions continues to be largely administratively determined whereas the demand for credit is determined by negative rates of interest and is accordingly unlimited, creating a serious disequilibrium. Unsatisfied credit demand leads to financial disintermediation, with a growing informal black market for short-term credit. Larger firms, unable to obtain credit from commercial banks, are turning increasingly to the issuance of debentures, paying interest rates above commercial bank rates.

Imbalance between Supply and Demand. The emergence of 157 Funds was a great boost to the development of demand in the market and a major reason for the eventual crash in 1971. The experience in Brazil emphasizes the importance of a balanced program of supply and demand incentives to allow the market to grow properly.

Inflation. A major detriment to capital market development is inflation. Inflation is basically the result of a struggle for the distribution of income between the different sectors of the community, initiated as often as not by the desire of the state to spend above its limits, or in other words, to spend in violation of market conditions.[2] Inflation affects equity market development through the relative price of capital, the allocation of financial resources, the real rate of return of enterprises, and the effects on productivity. Although indexed assets are beneficial to alleviating the problems of inflation, the historical experience of Brazil and other countries that have implemented indexation systems seems to uphold the assertion that indexation accelerates the rate of inflation.[3] In an article discussing the relationship between inflation and securities markets, Javier Fraga states:

> Hence, we may not strengthen capital (equity) markets by learning to live with inflation, nor by generating indexed instruments which will outlast inflation. The real need is to understand that inflation is the security market's worst specific microeconomic enemy.[4]

High Concentration of State-Owned Enterprises. Another detriment to equity market is the high concentration of state-owned enterprises. In addition to being able to obtain below-market interest rates, giving such firms advantage over private firms, state-owned enterprises often have a perceived business risk lower than private firms because the government is a major shareholder. Privatization of government enterprises not only will increase trading — and possibly the number of shareholders on the exchange — but also will increase government revenues by the sale of the equity.

Brazil's capital market development program in the 1960s had a great effect on the current development of the equity market today. Many authors attribute the depth and volume in the market, in spite of the current economic problems, to the programs initiated then.[5]

INDIA

India was chosen because it has a large geographical area with a large population, it is a culturally diverse nation, and it has a large functioning equity market (14 exchanges) without a strong central authority and without strong cross-exchange trading capabilities.

Historical Financial Framework

This section discusses the historical financial framework of India. Of the countries surveyed, only India has had a stock exchange in operation since 1875. India's financial framework can be divided into four stages: infant/growth stage, deterioration stage, dormant stage, and growth stage.

Infant/Growth Stage (1875–1946)

The stock exchange in India was established in 1875 to facilitate the negotiation of the sale and purchase of securities throughout the Presidency of Bombay. It followed the model of its colonial organizers, the British model, with its corresponding emphasis on exchange self-regulation, not necessarily on comprehensive securities legislation with a securities commission. It enjoyed a very liberalized environment, with market forces playing a major role in pricing issues. In this environment, the market grew and developed quickly, with various booms and busts, such as the bank failures in 1913, caused in part by the lack of proper regulation and oversight. Public interest in stock exchanges furthered, resulting in the opening of the Calcutta Exchange in 1908. With the beginning of World War I, Europe ceased to produce any articles except for war materials, which caused a boom for industrial enterprises in India. The market continued to grow until 1929 when the

U.S. equity market crashed. A world economic depression soon followed.

During World War II, a boom ensued, bringing unprecedented prosperity to the exchanges (six at that time). After a brief slump, the market again continued to grow. It reached a peak in 1946 but plunged after the Great Calcutta Killing, communal warfare, and widespread labor unrest.

Deterioration Stage (1947–1959)

Following independence, prominent Indian leaders were influenced by British socialism, which advocated government intervention to guide the economy, including public ownership of key industries. In 1948 a policy resolution gave the government a monopoly in armaments, atomic energy, and railroads, removing these areas from listing on the exchanges.

In addition to nationalizing industry, India inherited a competent civil service versed in administering controls from the British. By the late 1950s, controls were pervasive throughout the economy.

Government attitudes toward foreign investment were also changing. Whereas once the government was ambivalent to foreign investment, the attitude changed to one of limiting the expansion of foreign private investment, including making the distinction between foreigners and nonresident Indians (NRIs).

The Foreign Exchange Regulation Act (FERA) was passed in 1947 while the nation was recovering from the effects of World War II. It was a highly detailed piece of foreign exchange control legislation. It distinguished between foreigners and nonresident Indians and proscribed the allowable activities of each. Nonresident companies were a part of FERA, as were Indian companies with more than 40 percent of equity held by nonresidents, often referred to as FERA companies. As such they were liable to specific controls and regulations, including restrictions on investments in various industries and geographical areas and on equity investments in resident Indian corporations.

In 1956, the government continued its nationalization activities adding 17 industries exclusively for the public sector, including life insurance companies. The government wanted and obtained control of all the major areas that affected industry. Private companies were relegated to the production of noncritical consumer goods, and all areas of private-sector activities were set forth in the Companies Act of 1956.

The Companies Act detailed the structure and legal functioning of a limited liability company from its inception to its eventual demise. It is a comprehensive repertory of rules covering every conceivable aspect of an Indian company's existence, including the role and duties of management, constitution of the board of directors, and appointment and duties of auditors. The structure of the organization was similar to Western organizations, with one major difference. Regardless of whether the company was public or private, the government had extreme powers of oversight and intervention. Reporting requirements were much more extensive than those of many OECD countries. This law emphasized shareholders' rights and corporate democracy and deemphasized management rights. Shareholders' rights were vigorously protected, whether from dilution, from self-dealing by directors or management, or from limited or untimely communication of information.

Also during that time, the government emphasized special loans instead of raising funds through the securities markets. Commercial banks and development finance institutions provided priority sectors of industry with funds needed at below-market costs. However, although the Industrial Credit and Investment Corporation of India was supposedly private-sector oriented, there was no true private-sector development bank.

To maintain a greater control over the securities markets, an area where the government had only limited control, the Securities Contracts Regulation Act was enacted. This act governed the regulation of stock exchanges, trading practices, and the listing of securities on the exchanges. In each of these activities, the government reserved the right to intervene, and it did so actively. This resulted in a blend of government intervention that protected the existing structure and was, in many ways, harmful to true shareholder protection and progressive change in the system.

The law gave the government the power to formally recognize exchanges, with only government recognized stock exchanges, regardless of organization, allowed to trade securities; to intervene in any or all areas of the stock exchanges, to the extent of dissolving the exchange entirely or simply prohibiting further trading; to prohibit options of any sort; to force private firms to go public, while allowing tax concessions to public firms; to require that 40 percent of total equity of a listed firm be sold to the public, with the limitation that nonresident Indians and foreigners not hold more than 50 percent of the equity, except in special cases; and to require that shares for issues underwritten by brokers alone have a distribution of 20 shareholders for every 100,000 rupees of capital raised.

The stated aim of the Securities Contracts Act was to prevent undesirable transactions in securities by regulating trading and by stipulating the precise terms for transfer and settlement. However, in terms of investor protection, the act failed to address such important issues as accounting standards, deceptive trading practices, and insider trading.

Dormant Stage (1960–1973)

In the early 1960s, the government suspected private trading houses and conglomerates of manipulating markets and prices to their profit. Later, when shortages of goods were extensive, considerable criticism was leveled at traders for manipulating markets and prices. This led to the 1970s Monopolies and Restrictive Trading Practices Act (MRTP), which provided government with additional information, attempted to decrease the concentration of economic power through licensing, and placed constraints on certain business sectors deemed contrary to public interests.

The purpose of this act was to regulate the mergers and acquisitions of solely Indian companies in order to prevent situations of corporate monopoly and restraint of trade. The MRTP Act used a licensing system to control the growth and expansion of companies under its control. Without a license, companies could not operate and were essentially forced out of business.

This antiprivate-sector attitude continued throughout this stage. Banks were nationalized in 1969, further strengthening governments' control over industry but also removing a large portion of listings from the exchanges. General insurance was nationalized in 1973. Further attempts were made to promote the public sector, including high corporation tax, income tax, and wealth tax rates.

In 1973, the Foreign Exchange Regulations Act was considerably expanded to include additional restrictions on FERA companies, including further restrictions on physical expansion, further limitations on investments in equity capital, and restrictions on the physical infrastructure of FERA companies. Not surprisingly, as a result of the amendments, many FERA companies became domestic Indian companies by going public and increasing the number of outstanding shares to Indian residents. This provided a major stimulus to the equity market as domestic investors had the opportunity to buy shares of many well-run, profitable companies at attractive prices. This situation resulted in the market boom of 1974.

Growth Stage (1974–1988)

With the addition of shares of well-run FERA companies, the market began to grow once again. Added to this was the government's concern for financing its budget and its realization that having an efficient stock market could help alleviate the requirements of the corporate sector. Government attitudes toward the private sector began to change, from viewing the private sector as "bad" to "not safe, but not bad."

Growth continued, based on a highly speculative market with most large trades made outside the market. Pent-up energies, a highly volatile market, small float, and a trading market helped to move the market to new highs. Interest developed so much that five new stock exchanges were opened from 1978 to 1984.

In 1984 the government established a committee, headed by G. S. Patel, former head of the Unit Trust of India, to review the organization and functioning of all 14 stock exchanges. Major suggestions of the committee include establishing a high-powered body like the U.S. Securities and Exchange Commission,[6] recommendations that 50 percent of funds raised by public limited companies should be in the form of equity (hence affecting managements' leverage), encouraging institutional investors to become active sellers of equity, reducing time limitations on bonus issues, and reducing the capital gains holding period from three years to one year. Although some of the recommendations have been implemented, most have yet to be acted upon.

After a decade of slow economic growth, the government has started to modify its approach to regulating the economy. Liberalization of the economy is progressing, giving a needed boost to the market. However, controls were not dismantled, only loosened. By 1984 import regulations had been relaxed, licensing procedures were loosened and speeded up, more effort was made to attract foreign firms, prices of controlled commodities were raised, and controls on the expansion of firm capacity were relaxed, making production profitable and attracting private investment.

India is beginning to move toward the modern securities market stage. Recent legislation, effective since 1984, has made important changes. There is now annual auditing of stockbrokers. Previous legislation did not require annual auditing, and stock exchanges had limited powers to do so. Companies with capitalization above a required limit are required to file biannual reports, instead of annual reports only, giving more timely information to the government and investing public. Listing requirements were changed for non–FERA companies, which required 40 percent of the stock be offered to the public, with the amount offered being only 20 percent if the company made a second offering within the next three years, effectively allowing a grace period if current market conditions were not suitable. The rules regarding the issue of bonus shares were also relaxed, making it easier to offer bonus shares. In addition, All-India Institutions (major state-owned institutions such as the Industrial Development Bank of India, Industrial Finance Corporation of India, UTI, and GIC) agreed not to assist privately held companies unless they agreed to go public within a stipulated time period. Capital-gains tax on shares was cut, making shares a more attractive investment. These, and other legislation, contributed to the boom in the securities markets during 1985 and the gradual leveling off during 1986–1987.

Regulatory and Institutional Framework

India's financial system is characterized by its two major segments: an organized sector, which includes regulatory institutions, commercial banks, development and cooperative banks, the stock market, and nonfinancial institutions, such as insurance companies, and the traditional sector, also known as the informal credit market, which provides funds for small enterprises, farms, and consumption. This section discusses the regulatory and the institutional framework of the organized sector.

Regulatory Framework

The stock exchanges in India are regulated under the Securities Contract (Regulation) Act of 1956. Major regulatory institutions include the Reserve Bank of India and the Controller of Capital Issues.

The basic elements of the financial system were established during British rule. The ultimate authority is the Ministry of Finance (MOF) with its principal agent as the Reserve Bank of India (RBI), nationalized n 1949. The RBI is the Central Bank of the Indian financial system. It formulates and implements monetary and credit policy, functions as a banker's bank, manages the liquidity reserves of the credit institutions and supervises their operations, maintains the exchange value of the rupee, controls payments for international trade transactions, and regulates transactions in foreign exchange.

The Controller of Capital Issues (COCI) was first introduced as a measure to prevent the establishment or expansion of those industries that did not assist in the production of war materials or goods during World War II. This control has continued since then and is concerned with capital publicly issued in excess of a specified minimum. In 1959 this minimum was Rs500,000, in 1969 it was increased to Rs5 million, and in 1985 it was increased to Rs10 million. Issues below the limit do not require consent of the COCI. In addition, the COCI is also responsible for pricing all new issues, which it does based on mathematical formulas, not taking into account market forces.

Institutional Framework

The institutional framework in India is composed of merchant banks, commercial banks, All-India Institutions, the Unit Trust of India, and stock exchanges.

India does not have a history of merchant or investment banking similar to other Western nations. Commercial banking began as a support for trade and continued that function to well after independence. When it became mandatory for commercial banks to invest much of their reserves in government securities, the business of brokerage expanded to the role of brokerage houses.

With the growth in the equity markets during the past decade, the need for merchant banks as promoters and packagers of securities and financial services has grown. Merchant banks in India perform their major function of issue management, with additional legal and accounting functions of company and joint venture formation, Indianization, company deposits, and private placements.

In an attempt to increase the role of banks as catalytic agents of development, India nationalized the commercial banks. More than 90 percent of commercial bank assets are under government control, with the purpose of reducing banks' concentration of economic power and their influence on industrial and business monopolies and increasing the flow of credit to small business and industries. However, with this nationalization has come reduced profitability and decreased operational autonomy of management within the banks.

Since independence in 1947, several institutions have been established to provide long-term credit. Those institutions that operate on a national basis are referred to as All-India Institutions (AII). Principal All-India institutions are the Industrial Development Bank of India (IDBI), the Industrial Credit and Investment Corporation of India

(ICICI), Industrial Finance Corporation of India (IFCI), the Life Insurance Corporation of India (LIC), and the Unit Trust of India (UTI). These institutions work individually, and in consortium, to meet the financing requirements of the domestic companies in India.

The UTI dominates the capital market as a result of its monopoly status and its overwhelming size. It was established in 1963 as the sole financial intermediary for the sale and management of unit trusts (mutual funds) in India. UTI established a total of 14 different funds, one of which has since matured and been liquidated. Returns on UTI funds have been greater than on stock market indexes in general, partly because of its ability to buy equity directly from both individuals and financial institutions without having to go through the market and its ability to obtain lower-cost equity through its underwriting operations.

Investors in UTI benefit from tax advantages unavailable to the individual investor. A unit-linked Insurance Plan is operated in association with the state-owned Life Insurance Corporation and the General Insurance Corporation of India, providing a combination of investment returns, income tax deductions, and disability insurance coverage.

In addition, many UTI funds compete directly with bank deposits. Consequently, UTI attempts to offer unit holders with stable competitive rates. This has forced UTI to increase its fixed-income holdings, at the expense of equity investments.

Stock exchanges in India are regulated by the Securities Contracts Act of 1956. There are currently 14 stock exchanges within the country, with the Bombay Stock Exchange the largest. It accounts for about 60 percent of daily trading volume in India. Each exchange operates within the framework of its rules, bylaws, and regulations, which the government approves before granting recognition. Stock exchanges in India are organized as a voluntary, nonprofit-making association or as a public limited company by guarantee. There are very few companies listed on more than one exchange, with no linkages between exchanges.

Primary and Secondary Equity Markets

More aggressive marketing of stocks, recent stock market performance, successes of many new issues, and the growth of per capita income and savings have brought many new investors to the stock markets. There were about 7 million shareholders in India in 1985. In a survey of sample companies by the IDBI, individuals accounted for 31 percent of equity holdings, financial institutions for 24.7 percent, joint stock companies for 22.2 percent, and government entities for 20.4 percent.[7] Of these amounts, most individual investors, financial institutions, and joint stock companies invested the majority of their funds with private- and joint-sector companies; the majority of government entities funds were invested in public-sector companies. Most of the buying and selling orders emanate from individual investors whereas the volume of business in the market is clearly dominated by the institutions but executed off the exchanges.

The private sector, as well as the government, raises funds on the stock market. Individuals may buy shares in state-owned firms, although the government holds a controlling interest. An important aspect of the market in India is the overwhelming importance of government securities (both stocks and bonds) in the volume of operations as compared to industrial securities. During 1971–1972, new funds mobilized through the issue of government and semigovernment securities accounted for 93 percent to 97 percent of total new funds mobilized, with the remaining funds for the private corporate sector. Although the figures are very dated, there is still a high ratio of public- to private-sector funds raised in the equity markets in India.

Primary Markets

The volume of new equity issues in India is difficult to determine accurately as the COCI data indicate only that portion of amounts raised over the regulated floor. No estimates of data are available below the floor amount.

Although historically capital markets have played a minor role in the mobilization of capital for the private sector, a change is occurring. New equity issues in 1985 exceeded Rs21 billion, compared with Rs15.7 billion in 1984 and Rs8.3 billion in 1983, showing an increased role in the mobilization of capital.

The 1980–1981 boom was caused partially by the FERA Act of 1973, which effectively required foreign multinational to reduce their stakes in Indian subsidiaries to 40 percent. About 90 companies were forced to offer stock at artificially depressed prices set by the committee of Indian institutions.

The 1984–1985 boom was caused by the landslide victory of the Congress Party and the mandate given Rajiv Ghandi. Ghandi's party introduced a number of changes with respect to industrial policy and the development of the capital markets. Changes regarding the capital market included reducing corporate income tax from 55 percent to 50 percent and from 60 percent to 55 percent for listed and unlisted companies; additional depreciation allowances for plant and machinery; and introduction of import liberalization policies. The budget also contained proposals for tax reductions for individuals, with the marginal tax rate being reduced to 50 percent and the unearned income surcharge being abolished. These changes, along with the government's progress toward a more market-oriented economy, helped fuel the 1984–1985 boom.

In 1979–1980 about half of the equity raised was for new issues; in the period 1981–1985 this increased to about 60–70 percent. Pricing of the issues is done by the COCI, with pricing based on historical data; no account is taken of future earnings potential and industry or management capabilities.

New issues in India must be subscribed by investors. Because of the underpricing by the COCI, there is often a great oversubscription to the equity shares. Shares are then allocated to different investors, with successful applicants often making large overnight gains. This formula approach to pricing results in initial purchasers making a profit whereas subsequent buyers are likely to lose. This pattern gives the market the impression of a "gambling establishment," seriously hindering confidence in the system.

Secondary Market

Of the 14 stock exchanges in India, four are established on a temporary basis. The Bombay Exchange is the largest, comprising over 80 percent of the market capitalization. Statistics for India are found in Table 9.2 and Figure 9.2.

The Indian markets have performed well over the past decade. The Emerging Markets Database (EMDB) increased from 100 in 1975 to 677 in 1987 in dollar terms.[8] The largest gain, however, was in 1985 as the index nearly doubled.

Market capitalization in India increased from US$6 billion in 1980 to US$18.2 billion in June 1988. Domestic listings on all the exchanges have increased from 2,265 in 1980 (more than many developed country exchanges) to 6,017 in 1987, the largest of any developing country.

Because of the buy and hold strategies of the institutional investors, much of the volume in the markets is for speculative purposes. In addition, because of the problems in pricing issues, this view is further emphasized in the market.

Equities may be purchased on margin in India. In addition, it is possible to buy shares for a 14-day period with no margin payment. This

TABLE 9.2
India Market Statistics — Currency Amounts in Millions

	1985	1986	1987 Q1	1987 Q2	1987 Q3	1987 Q4	1988 Q1	1988 Q2	1988 Q3
A. NUMBER OF LISTED COMPANIES									
Bombay Stock Exchange	1,529	1,912	1,995	2,062	2,148	2,106	2,151	2,183	2,210
B. MARKET CAPITALIZATION									
1) In Rupees	174,750	178,300	-	172,775	206,198	186,650*	195,846	256,569	318,791
2) In US Dollars	14,364	13,588	-	13,358	15,739	14,480	15,065	18,222	22,001
C. TRADING VALUE									
1) In Rupees**	61,340	135,960*	4,821	4,059	12,849	15,366	13,621	39,682	38,229
2) In US Dollars	4,959	10,781	370	317	985	1,182	1,044	2,949	2,680
3) Turnover Ratio	35.1	76.3	-	2.3	6.2	7.5	7.0	15.5	12.0
D. LOCAL INDEX									
1) F.E Bombay Index (1979=100)	396.4	424.8	414.6	379.1	395.8	389.9	379.0	451.2	566.8
2) Change in Index (%)	98.4	7.2	-2.4	-8.6	4.4	-1.5	-2.8	19.0	25.6
E. EMERGING MARKETS DATA BASE									
1) Number of Stocks in EMDB Sample	25	47	40	40	40	40	40	40	40
2) EMDB Share of Market Cap. (%)	27.6	45.9	-	33.3	28.9	36.6	34.0	41.1	38.1
3) EMDB Total Returns Index(Dec/84=100)	205.1	199.3	192.9	159.2	164.0	168.8	149.6	212.6	238.7
4) Change in EMDB Index(%)	105.1	-2.8	-3.2	-17.5	3.0	2.9	-11.4	42.1	12.3
F. EXCHANGE RATES									
1) Exchange Rates (End of Period)	12.1655	13.1220	12.9280	12.9340	13.1010	12.8900	13.0000	14.0800	14.4900
2) Exchange Rates (Average of Period)	12.3687	12.6110	13.0150	12.8093	13.0490	13.0000	13.0430	13.4557	14.2643

*Revised

**Cash settlement basis in 1987 and 1988.

Source: Quarterly Review, 46.

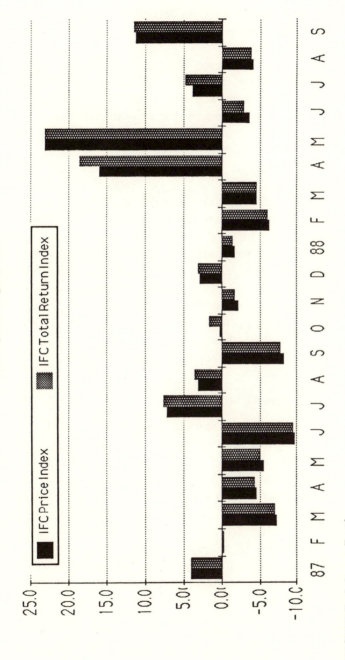

Monthly Performance Since January 1987
Monthly % Change in US$

■ IFC Price Index   ▨ IFC Total Return Index

FIGURE 9.2 — India

Source: Quarterly Review, 47.

is similar to buying an option without a cash payment or a futures contract without a margin. Further, because of the inability of the government to monitor brokers, brokers often buy stocks with no margin money paid to the exchange and without fear of action by fellow brokers on the exchange.

Brokerage in India is done by either individuals or partnerships, without limited liability. This is a holdover from the British system, which assumed that brokers would perform more in the public interest if they were not allowed limited liability status. This ruling leads, understandably, to undercapitalization. As most brokerage houses are undercapitalized, and with no investor protection against defaulting brokers, the possibility for a great loss of confidence through a domino effect is apparent.

Shareholder protection codes in India are not very effective. Recent legislation has been implemented to require equal terms when control changes hands. There are no written guidelines or regulations with regard to insider trading and share transactions by individuals or companies with privileged or price-sensitive information. There are also no restrictions on the directors' freely dealing in shares belonging to them or to their companies, except that under general law no officer is entitled to use insider information to his own advantage. In addition, there is no stock exchange compensation fund to reimburse shareholders who may be the victims of fraud or default by a market broker or trader.

Supply and Demand for Equity

The supply of securities comprises newly issued and existing securities. The former represents an additional resource mobilization through the securities market whereas the latter represents a transfer of resources among the shareholding public. In the Indian context, resource mobilization takes place mainly through rights issues for existing companies and new listings for companies entering the market for the first time. Bonus shares (resulting from retained earnings or revaluation of fixed assets) and secondary offerings of shares (for ownership restructuring or other purposes) do not involve additional resource mobilization but do affect the mobility of capital and the supply of corporate securities.

Supply of Equities

India has the largest number of listed firms of any developing country, and it is comparable to many developed countries. However, despite this large number of listings, only a small portion of the firms able to go public actually do so. Despite the limited availability of established, well-run companies and the probable demand for their equity if issued, many firms still are unwilling to go public for five major reasons. First, the effective cost of equity is significantly higher than is debt. Dividends are paid out of posttax profits whereas interest on loans is tax deductible; loans may be obtained at subsidized rates; and corporate short-term deposits from the public are a more attractive means of raising funds as there are no restrictive provisions. Second, family-controlled firms are unwilling to enlarge the capital base for fear of losing control. Third, the pricing of issues by the COCI usually results in well-managed companies priced much lower than market valuation, which acts as a damper to firms going public. Fourth, with the nationalization of a major sector, there is an absence of firms in the banking, insurance, and utilities sectors. Moreover, MRTP legislation has made it difficult for well-established firms to expand or diversify. And fifth, the possibility of a crowding-out effect resulting from the issue of public-sector debt securities with special features, with which the private sector cannot compete, has reduced the supply of equities.

Demand for Equities

One of the main reasons for the lack of demand during the 1970s was the low return on equity. Returns in later periods followed the same pattern. Returns on equity averaged about 13 percent while debentures provided a guaranteed return of 15 percent.

Institutional Investors

One of the trends in developed and developing country markets is the move toward the increasing proportion of securities held by institutional versus individual investors. Institutional investors are important as they provide a generally constant flow of funds to the market, provide a base of long-term investors in the market thereby increasing stability, and provide the resources to evaluate potential investments on a more professional basis than can the individual. Major institutional investors in India include the Unit Trust of India, the Life Insurance Corporation of India, the General Insurance Company, merchant banks, and mutual funds. Pension funds are not considered because they are required by law to invest only in government bonds.

The Unit Trust of India (UTI) is the sole financial intermediary for the sale and management of unit trusts (mutual funds) in India. It was established as a means of channeling individual savings into the stock market. UTI has over 1 million shareholders, with funds under management of about US$1 billion. Since the late 1970s, it is estimated that UTI has invested 50 percent in debentures and fixed deposits. This has limited its equity holdings because of the long gestation period and uncertain yield on new equity. In addition, UTI does not roll over its equity but prefers to hold it because UTI is compelled to distribute in the same year 90 percent of the income (defined as dividends and capital appreciation) earned during the year. Because UTI is concerned with steady, nonvolatile returns to its unit holders, it prefers not to book profits because it would then be compelled to distribute them. In addition, if it did sell its equity holdings, it would have to find alternative profitable investments; therefore, it follows the policy of only selling those shares where there is no expectation of capital appreciation.

UTI's performance has been very good over the years, probably because UTI buys equity directly from both financial institutions and individuals without going through the market and because it obtains securities in the process of its underwriting activities.

The Life Insurance Corporation of India (LIC) plays an important role in the capital market. It is one of the two most successful institutional investors in India. The LIC is required by law to invest 75 percent of its funds in government securities. This automatically limits the number of funds available to the private sector or the equity market. Of the remaining 25 percent, it is estimated that fewer than 3 percent of these funds are used for private-sector equity investing. The LIC is the most important institution for underwriting equity and debenture issues for the industrial sector.

The General Insurance Corporation (GIC) must invest 70 percent of annual additions to investable funds in "socially oriented" sectors: government securities, bonds and debentures of public-sector undertakings, and loans on soft terms to state governments and other agencies engaged in housing and urban development. Of Rs12.8 billion in investments in 1982, about one-half was invested in government securities, one-third in shares and debentures, term loans, and deposits with companies, and the remainder in loans to banks.

In addition to UTI, since 1983 several private unit trusts or mutual funds have been established in India. They are not yet significant when their total asset value is compared to UTI.

Indian institutional investors do not appear to trade their portfolios actively in the market. When major institutions and state financial institutions acquire shares, they often sell directly to UTI bypassing the market completely and causing a substantial loss of market liquidity and pricing information. As a result, most trading in the secondary market has been left to individual investors with a short-term, often speculative outlook. In addition, when institutions trade on the market, they buy and sell in large quantities, distorting the market and squeezing out private investors.

The government currently is thinking of relaxing legislation concerning mutual funds aimed at accelerating the pace of growth in the capital market, increasing competition, and providing a wider choice to investors. Mutual funds not only would mobilize larger resources for development but also could provide the basis for increased activity in secondary security markets.

Internationalization of the Equity Markets

India is attempting to open its securities markets to international portfolio investment by means of a phased liberalization program, comprising the initial stage and country fund stage. Further stages have yet to be announced. This section discusses the initial stage and the country fund stage.

Initial Stage (1947–1985)

In the initial stage, which first began with the FERA legislation in 1947, nonresident Indians (NRI), as well as persons of Indian origin, were permitted to make portfolio investments. On a repatriation basis, an NRI is permitted to invest in new equity and convertible debentures for up to 40 percent of new issues of manufacturing companies, hotels, and hospitals, similar to Indian investors. Previously, they were required to hold the shares for one year, but that restriction has been lifted. NRIs are also permitted to buy existing issues if one individual holds no more than 1 percent of capital and NRI investment does not exceed 5 percent of the capital of the company. NRIs are a clearly defined source of funds being targeted by merchant banks and brokerage houses.

Country Fund State (1986–Present)

The government recently decided to liberalize the market further and allow foreigners to make portfolio investments on a controlled and limited basis. Two funds have been approved and are currently investing in

India. The first is the India Fund, traded in London. The second is the India Growth Fund with Merrill Lynch as the lead manager. Other funds are proposed but not yet approved.

The funds benefit from the special tax-exempt status of the UTI and will be free from capital-gains tax; income will be taxed at 25 percent. No shares of the funds are sold or offered in India. Both funds invest mainly in Indian equity; the New York fund has the option to invest in U.S. securities on a temporary basis.

Major Development Patterns

The previous description and analysis shows that certain government actions fostered equity market development and others hindered its development. The next section discusses some of those actions.

Positive Development Factors

Government Guidance and Direction. The government is currently focusing on the importance of liberalizing and moving more toward a market-oriented economy and of developing the securities markets as a means of mobilizing funds for both the private and public sector. Recent reforms have increased investor confidence in the market and have stimulated securities market growth through greater confidence in the future.

The Patel Commission. In 1984 the government established a committee to review the organization and functioning of all 14 stock exchanges. The work has been completed and many of the suggestions have already been implemented. This type of study is important for any equity development program because it helps determine the state of the market and new goals. Such a study should be performed at regular intervals, approximately every five years.

Regulations to Assist Only Public Companies. The All-India Financial Institutions will assist only publicly owned companies and privately owned companies that agree to go public within a stipulated period. This is another method to increase the supply of equity shares available to the market.

Indigenization of Productive Activities. FERA regulation has been successful in limiting the amount of ownership in Indian companies. Because it has been a major goal of the government it is considered a positive factor, although it has probably been a detriment to overall equity market development.

Special Status of Nonresident Indians. India has mobilized, on a limited basis, foreign capital from nonresident Indians. This has been a boon to the equity market and has been a step toward the future internationalization of the market.

Negative Development Factors

High Corporate Tax Rates. High corporate taxation inhibits dividend distribution, which in turn discourages the investment of savings in the stock market. In addition, because dividends are subject to double taxation, wealthier shareholders subject to high marginal rates will prefer retention of profits by companies to the benefit of their own effective tax rate. The growth of retained earnings should lead to an appreciation of the shares, allowing capital gains taxable at a lower rate.

Requirements to Invest in Government Securities. The LIC of India is required to invest 75 percent of its assets in government securities. This severely limits the number of funds available to the equity market.

Buy and Hold Strategies of Institutional Investors. Institutional investors in India have a buy and hold strategy that limits secondary market development. This is so because UTI is compelled to distribute 90 percent of the income in the same year it is earned. Because UTI is concerned with steady, nonvolatile returns to its unit holders, it prefers not to book profits because it would have to distribute them. If it did sell its equity holdings, it would have to find alternative investments; therefore, it follows the policy of only selling those shares where there is no expectation of capital appreciation.

Assets held for less than three years are taxed as ordinary income; those held longer than three years are taxed as capital gains. Institutions are thus encouraged to use a buy and hold strategy.

Institutional Investors Bypass Secondary Market. None of the financial institutions appear to trade their portfolios actively in the secondary market. When major institutions and state financial institutions acquire shares, they often sell directly to the UTI, bypassing the market completely and causing a substantial loss of market liquidity and of market price equilibrium information.

Institutional Funds Competing with Bank Deposits. Many UTI funds compete directly with bank deposits. Consequently, UTI attempts to offer unit holders stable competitive rates of return. This has forced UTI to increase its fixed-income holdings at the expense of equity investments further depressing primary and secondary equity market performance.

Pension Funds Requirements. Pension funds in many countries are driving forces behind equity development. However, in India they are required to invest only in government bonds, further hindering equity market development.

Pricing of Public Issues. Instead of pricing at market rates for established issuers, the formula approach to pricing results in initial purchases making a profit. Subsequent buyers are more likely to lose. This system gives the market the impression of a "gambling establishment," seriously hindering confidence in the system.

Inadequate Monitoring of Brokers. Because the government is unable or unwilling to monitor brokers, brokers often buy stocks with no margin money paid to the exchange and without fear of action by fellow brokers on the exchange. Because most brokerage houses are undercapitalized and investors have no protection against defaulting brokers, the possibility for a great loss of confidence through a domino effect is apparent.

Subsidized Funds. The role of equity markets in India was limited during the 1960–1970s because commercial banks and development finance institutions provided subsidized funds to priority sectors of industry. Where equity markets compete with alternative sources of funds on an unequal basis, at below-market rates, the development of the equity market is handicapped.

Inadequate Margin Requirements. Because of inadequate or no margin requirements, one may buy shares for a 14-day period with no money down. This practice may lead to a large domino effect in a downward market, causing great loss of confidence and the ensuing harm to equity market development.

Private versus Public Placements. In 1983 more than half of the investments of UTI were in the form of private placements. Although a good way for UTI to make a profit, private placements hinder the proper development of the primary equity market.

High Concentration of Government Ownership. Nationalization of many industries and high concentration of government ownership of firms may eventually harm the market. Perceived risk on government-owned firms is less because of reduced bankruptcy and funding risks.

Lack of Investor Protection Code. The stated aim of the Securities Contracts Act is to prevent undesirable transactions in securities by regulating trading and stipulating the precise terms for transfer and settlement. However, in terms of investor protection the act fails to address such important issues as accounting standards, deceptive trading practices, insider trading, and insurance against brokerage firm nonperformance.

India is beginning to realize the importance of the private sector in mobilizing savings for both private- and public-sector development. Recent indications from government sources show the government taking a much broader and proprivate-sector view. This stand should benefit the private sector and the equity market.

KOREA

Korea was chosen because it has a very strong central government; it has a functioning equity market, large by Asian standards; and it has a systematic plan for internationalizing and liberalizing the Korean securities markets.

Historical Financial Framework

This section discusses the financial environment within which the Korean equity market has operated during the past two decades. It covers the infant, slow growth, rapid growth, and modern securities market stages.

Infant Stage (1953–1963)

As the post–Korean War restoration efforts subsided, the Korean government redirected its attention toward long-term economic growth. The government recognized very early the importance of securities markets in the efforts to mobilize domestic savings. This recognition resulted in passage of the Securities and Exchange Law of 1962. This law, similar to the U.S. Securities and Exchange Law of 1934, provided a legal framework on which to build an efficient and orderly market. The purpose of this law, as amended in 1976, was to contribute to the development of the national economy by attaining wide and orderly circulation of securities and by protecting investors through fair issuance, purchase, sale, or other securities transactions. However, the law was inadequate to change the existing stock market, characterized as a center for rigging, cornering, and speculating.

During 1961–1963, trading was dominated by common stocks of the Korea Stock Exchange and the Korea Securities Finance Corporation. Speculation ensued, influenced by the military takeover and the new government, which drove the stock market to new highs, fueled by more than 1,071 percent turnover that year. Correction followed, culminating in a market crash in February 1963. Share trading fell from 57.6 billion shares traded to barely over 300 million shares traded in 1964. The major damage from the crash was the loss of confidence in the stock market, the consequent suspicion, and avoidance of the markets. In addition, many private firms that might have gone public did not because of the stigma of having their share prices established by the whims of an uncertain market. This persistent negative public attitude toward the securities market was a significant factor leading to the continuation of a depressed market, a condition which some authors believe still has not been rectified.

Slow Growth Stage (1964–1971)

The crash hurt the market for several years, with many years of lackluster performance and unattractive yields for investors. After the First Five-Year Economic Development Plan took hold in the 1960s, the economy grew at double-digit rates, making a stronger securities system critical. As the demand for loans exceeded the supply, the government introduced the countermargin interest system, which required deposit rates to be higher than loan rates to maximize the inflow of personal savings to commercial banks.

The Law on Fostering the Capital Market was passed in 1968. It was to promote the sound development of the capital market by encouraging enterprises to go public, stimulating widely dispersed ownership of shares, and creating an investment climate ensuring the public's participation in enterprises and efficient raising of corporate funds. This law provided that should declared dividends be lower than a proscribed limit, dividend rates for government-held shares would be reduced to ensure proper returns for private investors. Securities could be listed as collateral or substitute for any guarantee money. The Minister of Finance was empowered to sell all or a portion of state-owned shares at a price lower than the prevailing market price, as long as selling achieved a broad dispersal of share ownership. The law also gave current employees of publicly held or listed corporations rights to 10 percent of total new shares. It gave a lower preferential treatment with regard to corporate income tax for publicly held firms, exempted interest and dividend income from any income tax, permitted preferential depreciation allowances for firms going public, and established the Korea Investment Corporation, which assumed responsibility for issuing market securities.

The next major law passed was the Securities Investment Trust Business Law in 1969. The objective of this law was to create a definite securities investment trust system and protect beneficiaries of securities investment trusts, thereby making easier ordinary investors' investments in securities and contributing to the efficient mobilization of industrial funds. This law was designed to encourage private investors to participate actively in the securities market. According to this law, only a contractual type of investment trust was to be established in Korea, rather than a corporate type of trust, such as mutual funds found in the United States. Limitations, unless approved by the Ministry of Finance, require that trusts invest no more than 10 percent of all trusted assets in the same security, invest no more than 20 percent of the total number of outstanding shares of a company, invest only in securities listed on the Korea Stock Exchange, and not invest in shares of the manager company. To meet the needs of different groups of beneficiaries, trust funds differ in the composition of assets, primarily consisting of stocks and bonds. Since their establishment, investment trusts have grown sharply, with most of the beneficiary certificates sold to small investors.

As a further impetus to the securities markets, the government lowered the rates on general bank deposits. By lowering the general bank interest rates, the gap between the deposit rates and securities yields was narrowed, making investments in securities more attractive. As a result of these laws and regulations, an increasing number of new investors began to participate in what had been a speculative market in the supply of long-term capital sorely needed by various industries.

Rapid Growth Stage (1972–1976)

Based on the fundamental improvement of the first two stages, and the success of the first two five-year plans (surpassing most of the specified goals), the securities market was well positioned for growth. However, three problems still existed: first, a huge unorganized money market, where small suppliers were able to realize higher yields than from other existing markets and to which demanders of funds were forced to turn because of lack of funds in traditional banking institutions; second, general bank deposit rates, considered less risky, in spite of lower yields; and third, the view of private firms that going public would not benefit future endeavors.

To rectify these problems, several important actions were taken. The Presidential Emergency Decree for Economic Stability and Growth was enacted in 1972. This decree froze all private loans to enterprises and rescheduled the interest rates at 1.35 percent per month, reduced interest rates on bank loans, and further reduced the corporate tax rate on publicly held firms. In addition, it required that all borrowing in the private money market be reported for legal rescheduling. Failure to report resulted in fines and the borrower was freed of all liabilities on the unreported amount of outstanding loans. In addition, a gift tax of 66 percent was assessed on loans illegally repaid. To further encourage reporting by lenders and borrowers, the decree exempted reporters from all tax liabilities that had not been paid as of the date of the respective reports. The primary effect of the decree was to reduce the interest burden by business enterprises by an estimated 20 billion won per year.

A second major provision allocated 200 billion won in order to assume a major portion of private loans made to specific industries. The last major provision lowered interest rates in both the banking and private money markets. The government, also aware of the implications on bank profitability, extended special loans to banking institutions to cover the losses from holding less profitable loan assets.

The next piece of major legislation was the Public Corporation Inducement Law enacted in 1974. Whereas the Law on Fostering the Capital Market emphasized advantages of going public, this law focused on measures to "induce," and where necessary, "force" companies to go public. The law established a Deliberation Council to analyze and decide on applicable policies; selected companies from an "eligible corporations list" and ordered them to go public (with certain exclusions); required firms to allocate preferentially up to 10 percent of common shares for employee purchase; and provided "special treatments" to those firms that had been designated to go public and to all firms that had already gone public. As a result of the law, 41 private firms went public during 1974. In addition, there was a large increase in the number of new offerings during that same period.

Although there was a significant increase in the number of firms going public, the number of public firms was only a small percentage of operating companies. Therefore, further government action was taken. The Presidential Special Instruction to the Cabinet of May 1974 provided additional incentives for private firms to go public. These incentives mostly considered guarantees for foreign loans and tax liability. In addition to offering incentives, it made operations more difficult for private firms by placing more stringent controls on the extension of bank credits for firms deciding not to go public.

Modern Securities Market (1977–Present)

The expansion of the securities market since 1968 can be attributed primarily to sustained government efforts for the development of the capital market and to active participation by the general public in the market. However, other problems relating to the rapid expansion and maintenance of an orderly and fair market arose.

To cope with these problems, the Securities and Exchange Law of 1962 was amended in 1976 to reorganize the regulatory structure of the securities market to strengthen administrative control and protect private investors, encourage the spreading of existing share ownership among more investors, regulate more strictly insider trading, and introduce a corporation registration system, separate from listing on the exchange.

In January 1981 the government announced a four-step program for the internationalization of the Korean securities market. The first phase of this plan was sales of beneficial certificates for overseas investors, begun in November 1981. This was the establishment of the US$15-million Korea International Trust (lead manager Credit Suisse First Boston) and Korea Trust (Merrill Lynch), both later increased to US$25 million. In late 1984 and early 1985, four new trust funds: the Korea Fund (First Boston, Shearson Lehman, and IFC), Korea Growth Trust (Jardine Fleming), Seoul International Trust (Baring Brothers and Vickers da Costa), and Seoul Trust (Prudential Bache) were also established. As of November 1988, all were trading with large premiums to net asset value.

The Securities and Exchange Law was amended again in 1982. Major changes were requirements of domestic and foreign securities firms to obtain approval from the Minister of Finance for conducting business in overseas or domestic markets, authorization of the SEC with the right to claim any undue profit from insider trading, and rights by shareholders who oppose a merger or takeover to put in a claim for purchase of their holdings.

In 1983, Measures for the Reinforcement of Capital Market Functions were enacted. Major changes included allowance of venture capital business to take part in the capital market, introduction of the issue-at-market price system, shifting of policy from a dividend rate system to a pay-out ratio system, and allowance of firms with 20 billion won capitalization to do new business in foreign markets.

During 1984, because of the lackluster market, only four companies issued equity at market prices. The issue-at-market price was revised in May 1985 in a bid to reinvigorate the rather depressed new issue market.

The revised system made it possible for more listed companies to issue new shares at market price by alleviating the requirements.

In June 1985, Measures for Fostering the Securities Market were announced. These included encouragement for individual investors and inducements of long-term capital by individual investors by granting tax benefits, expansion of securities investments by institutional investors, expansion of securities financing, and the requirement of fair and prompt disclosure of corporate information for the protection of general investors.

In November, the government announced Guidelines for the Floatation of Overseas Securities. Requirements of issuing corporations included net assets of 50 billion won or more and a base stock price above the weighted market average for all listed firms. Overseas issues need to be in the form of bonds convertible to equity. The conversion price must be above 110 percent of the equity price at time of the convertible issue, and conversion is not permitted within a year and a half from the issue date. However, the government still retained substantial control through a provision allowing this time to be lengthened. As of November 1988, only five companies, Samsung Electronics, Yukong, Daewoo Heavy Industries, Goldstar, and Saehan Media, had issued convertible bonds.

In December 1987 the government announced a series of measures to increase the liberalization process. Convertible bond investors were allowed to convert their holdings into underlying shares; however, the investors may retain the stocks or sell them on the domestic market, but they may not reinvest the proceeds on other Korean stocks or assign the converted stocks to other investors. Any of 20 eligible firms were permitted to issue overseas convertibles, if desired, and the Korea Europe Fund was allowed to increase capitalization to US$60 million.

In early 1988, Korea's current account was positive, which added a potential concern for the government — inflation. This added another important factor in speeding the liberalization process: mainly, changing the focus to how to curb the ample inflow of foreign capital from how to induce foreign capital. In line with this trend, in March 1988 the government announced new foreign exchange policy measures to induce investments in overseas securities as a preliminary step toward the ultimate liberalization of the Korean capital market. These included establishing an overseas fund for Koreans to invest in overseas securities, allowing securities companies to invest as much as US$30 million each in foreign securities, and allowing insurance companies and investment trust companies to hold up to US$10 million in foreign currencies.

The government of Korea realized very early the importance of the securities market to the mobilization and efficient allocation of domestic resources and made great strides in encouraging its development. It has pursued flexible and versatile strategies suited to the nation's current conditions. The next section discusses the regulatory and institutional framework of the equity market in Korea.

Regulatory and Institutional Framework

The financial system in Korea is divided into the modern and the traditional sectors, which work side by side. The modern sector comprises regulatory agencies, development institutions, and regulated financial institutions. The traditional sector consists of informal markets, kye's, private firms, the kerb market, and other gray market financial institutions. Although the government strongly controls the modern sector, the traditional sector of the economy is generally ignored. However, Korea has used the informal sectors as an indicator of whether current policies on interest and exchange rates corresponded with market forces. By watching this sector very closely, the Korean government has been able to control its exchange rate and interest rates, but within acceptable ranges to ensure distortions are not too great.

With a background of historical and economic factors, this section next discusses the regulatory and institutional framework of the modern sector in Korea. A discussion of the traditional sector must be left to future research.

Regulatory Framework

The Korean securities market is under the control and guidance of the Ministry of Finance (MOF), as are the other financial sectors, banking, insurance, and investment finance. The MOF sets major policies and makes major decisions. Under the guidance of the MOF, the Securities and Exchange Commission (SEC), an independent entity, acts as the principal regulatory institution covering a large range of supervisory functions of the securities business. The Securities Supervisory Board functions as the SEC's executive body in fulfilling its role. It oversees the Korea Stock Exchange and the Korean Securities Settlement Corporation. Additional important agencies include the Securities Finance Corporation and the Korea Securities Dealers Association.

The SEC makes decisions on major issues relating to the securities market, maintaining a fair and orderly market, and supervising securities institutions. Decisions are implemented by the Securities Supervisory Board (KSSB). Major functions include reviewing registration statements, supervising securities institutions, maintaining a fair and orderly trading market, regulating margin trading, guiding listed corporations on financial management, regulating proxy solicitation, regulating take-over bids and large acquisitions, and maintaining a high standard of accounting practice.

The Korea Stock Exchange (KSE), established in 1956, is a government-controlled special public corporation. It is two-thirds owned by the government, with membership limited to 30 companies (there are currently 25 members). Officers and staff of securities companies are not eligible to become KSE board members or officers. The Korea Securities Settlement Corporation (KSSC) is a wholly owned subsidiary of the KSE and performs settlement functions for the exchange.

The Securities Finance Corporation (KFC) provides securities financing to both underwriters and investors for the acquisition or (short) sale of listed securities. It also extends working capital loans collateralized by securities to securities companies.

The Korea Securities Dealers Association (KSDA) is a self-regulatory membership organization representing the interests of the securities industry, with all securities companies as members. Its main business includes public relations activities concerning securities investment, mediating conflicts between members, and training employees of securities companies.

Institutional Framework

Major financial institutions in Korea include commercial banks, special banks, and other nonbank financial institutions, such as merchant banks, securities companies, and investment trust companies.

Commercial banks in Korea may be divided into three categories: nationwide city banks, local banks, and foreign banks. All are characterized by conducting banking activities on a nationwide basis; by engaging in long-term finance (as well as normal short-term banking operations), usually by rolling over short-term loans or by purchasing bonds of long-term financing institutions; by being continuously short of funds and heavy borrowers from the Bank of Korea, partly because demand is so great and reserve requirements are so high; and by reporting large losses, which are usually covered by the Bank of Korea in the form of interest on deposits, because of the rigid interest rate structure encountered in Korea.

Nationwide banks have headquarters in Seoul but operate branches throughout the country. The government, until 1982, held a large proportion of the shares in four of these banks and exerted considerable influence. Although they have since sold their shares to the private sector, the government still has considerable influence with the banks. Nationwide banks' time and savings deposits account for more than 60 percent of the commercial banks' total financial resources, with 11 percent borrowed from the central bank.

Local banks are all privately owned. They account for 16 percent of outstanding deposits and 14 percent of outstanding loans of commercial bank business.

Foreign banks' deposits account for about 13 percent of outstanding deposits. About 70 percent of the funds of foreign banks are represented by borrowing from their head offices as they are not allowed to borrow from the Bank of Korea, except for swap transactions within prescribed limits.

Special banks have been established to fulfill special financial functions. They play an important role in the Korean banking system. They are directed and supervised by the government and receive some of their funds directly from the government. Examples include the Korean Development Bank, the Medium Industry Bank, the Export-Import Bank, and the Citizen's National Bank.

Other financial intermediaries channel savings to the business sector. These include merchant banks, securities companies, investment trust companies, and insurance companies.

Merchant banks provide corporate banking services, such as issuing securities, bill discounting, project finance, foreign currency loans, leasing, export financing, and term demand deposit taking. In practice, many of the merchant banking services in Korea are provided out of Hong Kong.

Securities companies are joint stock corporations that have obtained business licenses from the Minister of Finance. Securities companies, depending on capital size, engage in underwriting and buying and selling securities for their own account as a broker, intermediary, or agent.

As a general rule, business organizations other than securities companies are excluded from securities business. However, banks, trust companies, short-term finance companies, or merchant banks may engage in securities business by obtaining a license from the Minister of

Finance. Securities firms planning to expand abroad or foreign firms establishing a domestic presence also require prior approval from the Minister of Finance.

Investment trust companies are exclusively contractual, based on the trust contracts between the trust company and trustees, and act as both manager and distributor of the fund. There are three securities investment trust companies and six merchant banks involved in this business.

Following this presentation of the regulatory and institutional framework in Korea, the next section discusses the primary and secondary markets.

Primary and Secondary Equity Markets

The Korean Stock Exchange is the only trading floor in the country. It is 68 percent owned by the government. The remainder is owned by the 25 securities companies allowed to trade on it. It is one of the most modern exchanges in Asia with a high degree of computerization and a central depository system.

Individuals constitute the largest group of shareholders in Korean equities, owning more than half the shares. However, this can be misleading because 1 percent of the shareholders own more than 90 percent of aggregate market value.[9] At the end of 1985, there were 772,000 shareholders, representing 1 percent of the total population.

Primary Market

Primary shares in Korea are issued in two ways: issuing for consideration and issuing without consideration. The difference is in whether payment is required with respect to a new share issue. In most cases, stocks are to be issued at par. However, an exception exists for corporations incorporated more than two years and with the approval of the court and a special resolution of the stockholders' meeting.

Issuing new shares for consideration occurs when a corporation invites shareholders of record or nonshareholders to subscribe to its new shares, with payments in cash or other methods proscribed by the board. Corporations in need of capital would use this method as it includes payments in cash for shares. Selling these new issues is accomplished by granting rights offerings to current shareholders and granting subscription rights to special groups.

Before 1984, new issues had to be sold at par value, regardless of the prevailing stock price. Because of this regulation, issues for consideration seldom utilized a public offering. A public offering was mostly used in the case of establishing a new corporation or for firms deciding to go public. However, after establishing an issue-at-market price system, issues for consideration may yet be used for new offerings.

Issuing new shares without consideration is the method whereby the corporation increases the capital stock without any receipt in cash or other means of payment. New issues are distributed to shareholders of record in proportion to their share ownership, usually by the transfer of legal assets or asset revaluation reserves (retained earnings and capital reserves) to capital stock. The effect of this distribution is the same as that of the stock dividend often practiced by U.S. firms.

Before 1984, all new issues in Korea were sold at par, so the risk of price fluctuations was noticeably absent. Furthermore, because in most instances the par value of a firm was substantially less than the theoretical or market value of shares, the risk of not being able to sell the shares was minimal. Hence, underwriting was essentially a two-step process: the financing stage, the exchange of cash for securities, and the distribution stage, the selling of securities to investors. In most cases these were done by the same underwriter. Since the issue-at-market price was begun, the major difference has been the increase in risk of price fluctuation.

Secondary Market

Although the number of listings on the KSE at the end of 1985 was almost identical to total listings five years earlier, total market value in monetary terms had more than doubled. Listings on the Korean stock exchange increased from 189 in 1975 to 389 in 1987. Market capitalization in 1987 was US$32.9 billion, a nine-fold nominal increase over 1980 capitalization of $3.8 billion. Volume has also increased dramatically. Volume in 1975 was 334 billion won, which increased to 1,134 billion won in 1980 and to 5,693 billion won in 1987. Statistics for the Korean market are found in Table 9.3 and Figure 9.3.

As measures of performance, the Korea stock index rose from 90 in 1975 to 412 in 1987 (January 1980 = 100) in Korean won terms. The Emerging Markets Database of the International Finance Corporation, another important indicator of market performance of major actively traded stocks, increased from 100 in 1975 (December 1975 = 100) to 1,940 in 1987 in U.S. dollar terms. Overall, the market has performed better than the Standard and Poor's 500 and the Capital International Index in each of the past ten years (see Table 7.4 for comparative values).

TABLE 9.3
Korea Market Statistics — Currency Amounts in Millions

	1985	1986	1987 Q1	1987 Q2	1987 Q3	1987 Q4	1988 Q1	1988 Q2	1988 Q3
A. NUMBER OF LISTED COMPANIES									
Korea Stock Exchange	342	355	357	365	379	389	406	429	471
B. MARKET CAPITALIZATION									
1) In Won	6,570,403	11,994,200	18,126,809	18,925,080	22,430,588	26,163,050	31,992,830	41,879,561	45,139,941
2) In US Dollars	7,381	13,924	21,404	23,396	27,836	32,905	42,612	57,472	63,009
C. TRADING VALUE									
1) In Won	3,620,600	9,597,965	4,276,903	3,530,861	6,996,441	5,693,239	12,565,691	11,811,893	10,745,013
2) In US Dollars	4,162	10,889	4,998	4,296	8,664	7,123	16,288	15,978	14,868
3) Turnover Ratio	55.1	80.0	23.6	18.7	31.2	21.8	39.3	28.2	23.8
D. LOCAL INDEX									
1) KSE Composite Index. (Jan. 1980=100)	163.4	272.6	405.1	411.8	485.3	525.1	656.5	702.8	677.5
2) Change in Index (%)	14.7	66.9	48.6	1.6	17.9	8.2	25.0	7.1	-3.6
E. EMERGING MARKETS DATA BASE									
1) Number of Stocks in EMDB Sample	25	23	23	23	23	23	23	42	62
2) EMDB Share of Market Cap. (%)	32.5	39.3	30.3	28.0	26.0	24.4	24.4	43.5	61.8
3) EMDB Total Returns Index(Dec/84=100)	138.5	260.8	320.3	322.4	341.2	365.4	482.3	548.3	562.5
4) Change in EMDB Index(%)	38.5	88.3	22.8	0.7	5.8	7.1	32.0	13.7	2.6
F. EXCHANGE RATES									
1) Exchange Rates (End of Period)	890.1999	861.4000	846.8999	808.9000	805.8000	795.1000	750.8000	728.7000	716.4000
2) Exchange Rates (Average of Period)	870.0197	881.4500	855.6899	821.9000	807.5400	799.2400	771.4633	739.2786	722.6821

Source: Quarterly Review, 48.

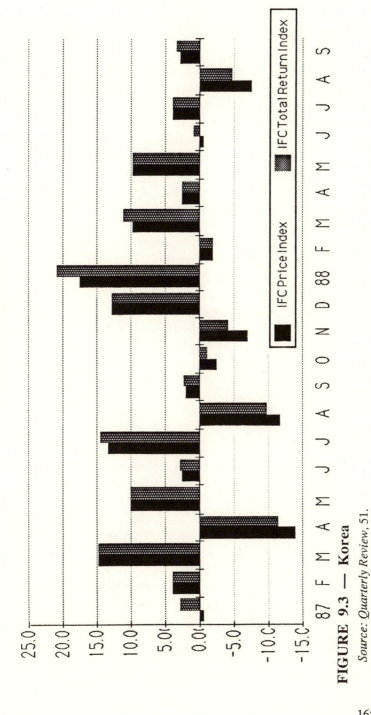

Monthly Performance Since January 1987
Monthly % Change in US$

FIGURE 9.3 — Korea

Source: Quarterly Review, 51.

Transactions outside the exchange floor are permitted for securities issued by registered or listed corporations. The OTC market uses negotiated transactions prices while the exchange is an auction market. OTC trading in Korea is significant, especially for bonds, with almost 50 percent of transactions on the OTC market.

Margin transactions were introduced in 1977 as a means of creating temporary supply and demand. A margin transaction is a purchase or sale of securities with credit (a part of the cash or shares needed in clearing margin transactions) in which securities companies extend credit or lend shares to their customers to enable them to settle transactions. Securities credit in Korea includes credit extended by securities companies, credit extended by the Korea Securities Finance Corporation (KSFC) to underwriting companies, securities collateral loans by the KSFC to KSE members and securities investment trust companies, and securities collateral loans by the KSFC or securities companies to public investors. The SEC strictly regulates the credit extension system by adjusting the rate of the down payment. At present, the margin requirement is 40 percent of the transaction value. Securities may be used as collateral for down payments and are assessed at 70 percent of market value for stocks, 90 percent for bonds.[10] In addition, if a securities company faces a shortage of funds or stocks, it can obtain a margin loan from the KSFC.

Supply and Demand for Equity

Supply of Equity

Many factors inhibit the supply of equity in Korea. These include the availability of alternative sources of funding, such as bank credit, kerb (unregulated) market financing, and corporate bond financing (which is guaranteed by financial institutions). Bank and corporate bond financing are at administered rates, often below market rates. Kerb market financing is at higher rates but is easily available and confidential.

Lack of incentives to go public also limit the supply of equity. The tax advantages accorded to public companies have been progressively diminished since 1979. Although in the long term the tax system should be neutral between listed and nonlisted companies, a temporary form of tax discrimination in favor of listed companies is justifiable in the interests of stimulating the development of the market. Although Korea has done well in expanding the supply of shares, many more companies could go public.

High costs of issuing equity has contributed to the lack of supply. In addition to the problem of new issues being sold only at par, regardless of the market value of the shares, the cost of raising funds through equity issues is more expensive than bank borrowing or bond issues. Finally, the traditional practice that dividend payout should move similar to time deposit rates has made equity returns similar to debt.

The underwriting system is ineffective in pricing and selling issues. Fees for underwriting and managing issues are fixed by the regulatory agency instead of being negotiated between the issues and management or underwriting group. And because many of the brokers are undercapitalized, they find it difficult to effectively make a market for the period after the issuance of equity, which is necessary to help promote confidence in the market.

Finally, as in most developing countries, companies in Korea fear loss of control of their companies. Related fears of having to release information about company activities to the public (including competitors and the government) prevent many from opening their companies to the public.

Demand for Equity

One of the major reasons for the lack of demand for equity has been the availability of higher-yielding (for the same risk) or lower-risk, (for the same return) investments. Kerb deposits and real estate investments have been controlled through high capital-gains taxes and other measures. Returns on corporate bond issues, guaranteed by the banks, have been generally higher with less risk, offering a more attractive investment, limiting the demand for shares.[11]

Investor protection in Korea is still limited, although better than in many developing countries. Reliable financial information is the heart of any investment decision. In addition, the view of market manipulation by the "big hands" (large investors) has reinforced the concept that the market is only for the larger investors.

Institutional Investors

The institutional market in Korea is only beginning to grow, but it already plays an important part in the market. Institutional investors provide a somewhat steady demand for equities, and they have been credited with reducing the costs of raising funds in the securities market.[12] As was seen in Figure 9.1, securities companies, investment trust companies, financial institutions, and insurance companies make up less than 21 percent of the share ownership in Korea. Major regulations have been passed that should encourage development of the institutional market with Korea. Institutional investors in Korea include investment trust companies, pension funds, and insurance companies. Generally, most of the institutions' assets are in bonds because of the lack of confidence in the equity market and the availability of higher returns and lower risk in the bond market.

Investment trust companies are the major institutional investors in Korea. Assets of the investment trust companies are predominantly in fixed-interest instruments, including those designated as equity funds. Investments by trust companies represent only a small portion of the total equity market, probably because of the lack of a successful history of performance and the general lack of confidence in the market. Currently nine institutions are authorized to undertake the management of funds, but only a few are active in the business.

Three major pension funds in Korea cover government workers, teachers, and the military. These funds are partially funded and partially financed by the budgets of the institutions concerned. Pension funds tend to have very little in their equity portfolios, probably because of their sensitivity to the possibility of capital loss, their lack of understanding regarding equity market operations, and their role as custodians of their members' pension rights.

Insurance companies are the second most important category of institutional investor. Much of their involvement in equities stems from requirements to invest in securities of companies in the government-determined priority sectors of industry. A large percentage of insurance companies' portfolios consist of loans to policy holders and small and medium-sized industries in the government-determined priority sectors. Of the remaining assets, fewer than half are in equities, with the majority in bonds.

Country funds, such as the Korea Fund, are a small but growing portion of the market, accounting for US$230 million in 1985. Foreign investors have shown a great interest in Korean securities because of higher returns and their low correlations with industrial markets.[13] These funds are discussed in greater detail in the next section of this case study.

Internationalization of the Equity Markets

Korea has been developing its financial system in pursuit of an open-economy system for ultimate liberalization of capital movement.[14] The government has established an underlying policy direction toward internationalization and liberalization of the securities market, which will be carried out in a step-by-step manner keeping abreast of the progress in foreign exchange and trade liberalization. Part of this liberalization program is the plan for internationalization of the securities markets.

Plan for Internationalization of the Markets

The plan for internationalization of the markets was first announced in 1981. It was divided into four stages, each covering specific periods and activities.

Stage One (1981–1984) was the indirect participation stage. As a first step, the government allowed two securities companies to establish investment trust funds in Europe and allowed a closed-end fund listed on the New York Stock Exchange, the Korea Fund, to invest in Korean securities. There are currently seven funds investing in Korea, three of which were established in 1985, with total capital of US$230 million.[15]

Stage Two (1985–) was the limited direct participation stage. With some quantitative restrictions, foreigners are allowed to purchase stocks directly. In addition, foreign investment houses are allowed to have representative offices in Korea. As part of this stage, Korean companies have been allowed to sell convertible bonds (CBs) in the Euromarkets. Following the successful floatation of the first Korean convertible bonds by Samsung Electronics Co., Ltd. in December 1985, other companies have also floated CBs in the Euro and Yankee bond markets. The most recent was Saehan Media in late 1988.

Stage Three (1988–) is the inward investment stage. Foreign investors will be allowed to invest freely on a reciprocity basis. Moreover, domestic funds will be allowed to raise equity funds in external markets with prior approval of the Ministry of Finance.

Stage Four (1990s) is the outward investment stage. At this point, the capital market is completely opened without any restrictions.

Korea currently is in stage two of the internationalization process. However, this stage has been extended, which will delay full internationalization until the late 1990s.

Of particular interest to foreign investors, in addition to convertible bonds, are country funds, such as the Korea Fund established in 1984. These are discussed next.

Country Funds

As a first step toward liberalization, the government allowed limited indirect investment in the stock market through mutual funds. As of December 1985, five open-ended and one close-ended mutual funds had started operations. The most significant of these was the Korea Fund with initial capital of US$40 million in 1984 and a second issue of US$60 million in 1986.

The Korean MOF has imposed "prudent restrictions" on the fund's operations to maintain stability in the securities market. It is prohibited from investing in more than 5 percent of a company's outstanding equity. It may not invest more than 25 percent of its assets in any one category of industry, and the turnover rate is limited to 50 percent. Although it is currently selling at a premium of 39 percent over net asset value because of a strong market performance, a more reasonable premium of 15 to 20 percent is expected. The Korea Fund was incorporated in Maryland and is sold on the New York Stock Exchange.

Convertible Bonds

In November 1985, the government announced Guidelines for the Floatation of Overseas Securities. This law gave guidelines whereby foreign investors are allowed to hold up to 15 percent of the paid-in capital of companies that issue CBs. A single foreigner, however, is allowed to hold only up to 3 percent of the paid-in capital of a single company. As of December 1985 Samsung Electric had issued convertible bonds, which were very enthusiastically received.[16]

Liberalization

McKinnon in 1973 characterized the Korean experience from 1964 to 1970 as "financial reform without tears." because the rise in nominal and real interest rates of banks not only had resulted in rapid growth of the banking system but also had apparently contributed to rapid growth of the whole economy.[17] In the 1980s, Korea has experienced liberalization and integration, not because of much real liberalizing of the banks, but because of more rapid growth in the less regulated nonbank financial sector. This may well be an easier route than freeing up the whole system in one stroke, as many countries have tried to do.[18]

Exporting Financial Expertise

As a beginning for the outward investment stage, Korea has begun exporting, in addition to goods and services, financial expertise, a much more advanced product.[19] As countries develop this financial expertise domestically, opportunities exist to market this expertise abroad, which Korea is doing.

Major Development Patterns

Much can be learned from an analysis of the development of the equity market in Korea. Many good and innovative ideas were encouraged, in addition to basic economic concepts that were followed throughout the market's development. Major development factors are discussed in this section.

Positive Development Factors

Government Action as a Development Agency. The most important force behind equity market development in Korea has been the Korean government. It is a good example of a government dedicated to developing the securities markets. Although there have been some problems in its development, overall the government has promoted equity growth. In addition to providing incentives for the market's development, it has eliminated disincentives to market growth.

Securities as Collateral. Securities are allowed as collateral or a substitute for any guarantee money or deposit to be furnished to the local or federal government entities or enterprises. This provides added liquidity to securities' investors, increasing attractiveness and demand.

Selling Government Shares at Below-Market Prices to Disperse Ownership. One of the unique characteristics of Korean companies is that a few insiders hold the vast majority of shares. The provision to sell government-held shares at below-market prices is an attempt to increase the number of minority shareholders. The government has shown its willingness to take a reduced profit in the short term to achieve a major long-term goal, development of the securities markets.

Lower Tax Rates for Publicly Held Firms. As an incentive to go public, the tax rates were decreased from 51 percent for private firms to between 38 percent and 45 percent, depending on ownership of the controlling shareholders.

Lowering General Deposit Rates. By lowering the general bank deposit rates, the gap between securities yields and deposit rates was narrowed, making securities investments more attractive.

Legislation Requiring Firms to Go Public. Government requirements to go public caused a substantial increase in the number of listed companies in Korea, from 66 in 1972 to 356 in 1978. The supply of equity was substantially increased.

Plan for Internationalization and Liberalization of the Markets. The Korean government has long realized the importance of the equity market to the development of the economy. It also realizes the importance of internationalizing the markets. By establishing a plan with a gradual time frame, it will allow the orderly expansion from a purely domestic to a truly international market.

Margin Transactions. The ability to purchase stocks on margin is a means of creating temporary demand, which may aid market development.

Sale of Government Shares in Existing Enterprises. The purchase and subsequent sale of shares in existing enterprises is a means of creating temporary demand and supply for shares. In addition, it allows the government to share initial startup risk when equity markets are not sufficiently developed.

Establishment of a Self-Regulatory Securities Agency. The KSDA was established to contribute to the sound development of the securities industry, which it has done.

Five-Year Plans and Market Development. As has been true of the past two five-year plans, the Sixth Five-Year Plan (1987–1991) has specific goals and objectives regarding the capital market, including domestic savings ratios, overseas savings ratios, and total investment ratios. This indicates the importance that the government places on the development of the market in Korea.

Concern for the Small Investor. The Korean government has shown great concern about the needs of the small investors in the attempt to diversify ownership. This has been evident from the legislation and emphasis the government has placed on increasing the number of shareholders. This should lead to better decisions by the companies as they will be concerned with overall investor welfare versus their own individual welfare.

Negative Development Factors

Existence of Unorganized Money Market. The existence of a large unorganized money market hinders equity market development. It attracts both suppliers and demanders of funds that might have utilized the securities market.

Loss of Confidence. A major result of the market crash of 1963 was the loss of confidence in the stock market. Not only did this cause a continuation of a depressed market. It also gave investors and potential firms a negative public attitude toward the market. It is taking years to overcome this feeling.

High Concentration of Ownership. With more than 90 percent of the market value of equities being owned by 1 percent of the shareholders, major shareholders possibly can employ manipulative practices.

The case studies follow the development of equity markets in three different countries. Because of their differences in history, culture, and governments, the paths taken have led to different types of financial systems and equity markets, although there is much in common among them. Moreover, much gleaned from the analysis of these markets may be relevant to the development of equity markets in other countries.

NOTES

1. Roberto Teixeira da Costa, *Brazil's Experience in Creating a Capital Market* (San Paulo: BOVESPA, 1985), 23.

2. Javier Gonzalez Fraga, "The Impact of Inflation on Securities Markets," in Nicholas Bruck, ed., *Capital Markets under Inflation* (Buenos Aires: Stock Exchange of Buenos Aires, Argentina, 1982), 339.

3. Arnaldo T. Musich, "Inflation in Brazil," comment on paper by Jorje Del Canto, "Impact of Inflation on the Development of Capital Markets in Argentina and Brazil," in Nicholas Bruck, ed. *Capital Markets,* 187.

4. Javier Gonzalez Fraga, in Bruck, ed., *Capital Markets,* 339–66. This article has an excellent discussion of the effects of inflation on securities markets.

5. See van Agtmael, *Emerging Securities Markets,* 1984, and da Costa, *Brazil's Experience,* 1985.

6. This has been rejected in place of a less powerful authority, which is understandable in light of the current experience of excessive regulation in all other sectors of industry and the concern that it would spill over into the stock exchange.

7. *GT Guide to World Equity Markets* (London: Euromoney Publications, 1985), 115.

8. The S&P 500 was at 472, the Morgan Stanley Capital International Index at 660 with December 1975 = 100 (see Table 7.4).

9. Alex Anckonie and Chang-hyun Chi, "Internationalization of the Korean Stock Market," paper presented at the Korea Economic Institute of America Meeting, November 5, 1986, 9.

10. *Major Listed Companies of Korea* (Seoul, Korea: Ssangyong Investment Company, June 1986), 121.

11.   Yoon Je Cho, "On the Liberalization of the Financial System and Efficiency of Capital Allocation under Uncertainty," Ph.D. dissertation, Stanford University, 1984.

12.   *Korea: Development in a Global Context* (Washington, D.C.: World Bank Country Study, 1984), 80.

13.   Correlation of the EMDB sample from Korea with the S&P 500 in 1985 was 0.28 on a U.S.-dollar basis.

14.   *The Securities Market in Korea* (Seoul, Korea: Securities and Exchange Commission, 1983).

15.   For a list of these funds, including value, date, and type, see *GT Guide to World Equity Markets,* 159.

16.   "Equity-tied Issue Is First in Euromarket for South Korean Firm," *The Wall Street Journal,* December 4, 1985, 47.

17.   Ronald McKinnon, *Money and Capital in Economic Development* (Washington, D.C.: The Brookings Institute, 1973).

18.   Yoon Je Cho, "The Role of the Financial Sector in Korea's Structural Adjustment," paper presented at the Conference on Structural Adjustment in a Newly Industrialized Country: Lessons from Korea on June 17–18, 1986 at Washington, D.C.

19.   Byung-Soo Lee, "Financial Companies Expand into Egypt," *Korea Business World* (March 1986), 15.

10

Summary and Conclusions

Financial sector work in DCs should respond to specific development objectives, i.e., contributing to faster, sustainable, and socially equitable economic growth. It involves creating many different types of public and private financial institutions and instruments. This ensures a reasonable distribution of savings among short-term instruments (deposit type or money market) and long-term debt (bonds) and risk capital (stocks and equity-related instruments) to meet the overall financing needs of the country and the individual risk and time preferences of individual investors.

However, many developing countries have only a bank-centered financial system. Although possibly appropriate in the past, this type of financial system cannot meet the current short- and long-term financing needs of developing countries and investors. As a monopoly source of funds, it is averse to establishing competition with other types of financial institutions (intrasectoral competition), and it cannot provide the long-term debt and risk capital so urgently needed. The next step should be a movement toward a more balanced financial institution.

Governments have also resisted the creation of additional financial markets. From a position of monopoly on fund mobilization, it is difficult to give up that position. The prospect of competing with the private sector for funds, especially during current high deficit conditions, does not appeal to many DC governments, although it is in the best interest of the country and government to do so. What has been needed is a better understanding of the theory, benefits, and costs of equity markets in developing countries. This book has provided part of that understanding.

Governments affect savings behavior through various fiscal, monetary, and economic policies. In theory, government-induced influences that operate on savings behavior should not be haphazard but should be the result of carefully thought-out public policies aimed at clear public interest objectives. In many DCs this has not been the case. Some government-induced influences do not appear to have been clearly thought out but were short-term responses to meet short-term objectives. This book has provided a clearer understanding of the necessary conditions for the development of an equity market to allow a better understanding of the cause and effect relationship of government-induced influences.

Ideally, the allocative influence of government-induced policies should be zero, but this is unlikely in the real world. Governments should attempt to minimize the distortions originating from haphazard government-induced influences to achieve some measure of equity in the mobilization and management of savings. This is not to say that allocative influences are necessarily bad. These same influences can be used very beneficially as tools to aid the evolution of the financial system necessary to achieve specific goals and objectives of developing countries. Tools that would aid in the development of the supply and demand for equities were discussed.

There are various sectors in the financial system consisting of different types of institutions and oriented toward different purposes and time horizons, but there is only one pool of local savings. Often this is insufficient, given the current price of money measured in terms of the interest rate. But there is an additional pool of savings from other countries, looking for attractive returns, diversification, and good values. Tapping this source of funds may be a viable alternative for developing countries. Although many governments and individuals may be concerned about possible negative effects of foreign capital, various methods can be established to limit the perceived costs of foreign capital while enjoying the benefits. Those areas were discussed from both the local and international investors' viewpoint, as well as methods used in various DCs to internationalize their equity markets.

Examples of equity market development successes and problems are prevalent. However, little has been written specifically about equity market development and the result of various actions. This study attempted such a discussion.

This book offers three conclusions. First, equity market development must be part of an overall financial development program, not just an isolated component. It is not an end but rather a means to achieve country-specific goals and objectives. As such, benefits and costs of equity markets must be viewed in terms of the overall financial system, not just the equity market, to be placed in their proper perspective. In addition, equity market development, as part of an overall financial sector development plan, should be based on a conscious decision that financial markets are very important. It should be part of each country's short- and long-range plans. In addition, an on-going analysis of a country's financial markets should be undertaken at least every five years.

Second, the effect of government policy actions on the development of the equity markets is readily apparent and discernible. Problems generally occur, not because the effects were unknown, but because policy actions were not thought through to their logical conclusion. Only a single viewpoint or objective was taken (usually the government's view). A major message is the importance of the private-sector communication with government in the development of equity markets and equity market policy decisions. Private-sector dialogue is important, not just in the initial stages of development, but in all stages of development. The attitude of the government toward the private sector appears to be a major factor in the success of any equity market development program.

Third, equity market development is a long-term undertaking, difficult, complex, challenging, but somewhat predictable. It is not the type of project that can be initiated one year and have the benefits materialize the next. Equity market development is a long-term undertaking and requires a corresponding long-term commitment. Therefore, development of the areas discussed in this research should be a concern of all governments regardless of the current state of the economy or the equity market. Moreover, the periodic review of the goals and objectives of any development program, even after the markets are well established, is important to maintaining the benefits discussed.

Equity markets are important to the financial and economic development of a country. The stage in a country's development at which an equity market should be established was not addressed; however, all countries should be developing the necessary political, economic, legal, institutional, and regulatory environments important for the successful development of an equity market. In addition, they should develop reasonable government policies regarding interest rates, exchange rates, taxation, institutional investors, and foreign participation policies that take into account the overall goals and objectives of the economy and that look to the long-term development of an equity market.

The development of equity markets in developing countries (or perhaps, in the short-term, greater development of the environment in which the market operates) is a very viable alternative and should be actively encouraged. Recommendations have been advanced that may boost the development of equity markets in developing countries. This book supports a gradual and interventionist approach to the development of equity markets in developing countries.

The importance of work such as that done by the IFC in financial system development, the recent capital markets study by the Asian Development Bank, and work by other private- and public-sector organizations is also apparent. These projects help educate investors about the benefits and costs of investing in these markets, make them more aware of investing in these markets, and aid in the development of the markets through discussions and work with developing country governments.

Data on developing country stock markets, such as the IFC Emerging Markets Database and the recent work by Morgan Stanley Capital International, Salomon Brothers, and Reuters, are also important. In addition to their educational aspect, they also allow important statistical work to be performed on markets where little work has been done. The development of databases by developing country markets should be an important priority for developing country governments. They supply additional data for important quantitative analysis necessary for market development.[1]

From a purely commercial view, this research has shown that these markets may be attractive to international investors. Although it is not a guarantee of future returns, developing countries have a very respectable history of high returns. Correlations with major markets are very low for all developing countries. Good values can be found in many developing countries because they have not yet been discovered by international and local institutional investors. Moreover, many of the problems in developing countries are being corrected: markets are becoming more liquid, disclosure has become surprisingly good, information has become more readily available, securities legislation has improved, investment restrictions have lowered, and taxes are being adjusted to international standards. For these reasons, equity markets in developing countries are becoming more attractive to international and local investors alike.

NOTE

1.   For an example of one type of analysis possible, see Bryan Sudweeks and Alex Anckonie, "Portfolio Implications of Investing in Developing Countries," paper presented at the 1987 AIB Conference, Chicago, November 1987.

Bibliography

Abrams, Richard K., and Donald V. Kimball, "U.S. Investment in Foreign Equity Markets," *Economic Review*. Federal Reserve Bank of Kansas City, April 1981, 17–31.

Adler, Michael, and Bernard Dumas. "International Portfolio Choice and Corporation Finance: A Synthesis," *Journal of Finance* 38 (June 1983): 925–84.

van Agtmael, Antoine. "DFI's: Moving toward a New Era in Development Finance." Speech given to the Association of Development Financing Institutions in Asia and the Pacific, April 24, 1986, Auckland, New Zealand.

____. *Emerging Securities Markets*. London: Euromoney Publications, 1984.

____. "Fiscal Policies in Securities Market Development." Presentation at the capital markets seminar in Lisbon, Portugal, May 12–13, 1983.

____. "Investment Opportunities for Japanese Institutions in Emerging Markets." International Finance Corporation (IFC), presented at the Japanese Center for International Finance, May 7, 1987.

van Agtmael, Antoine, and Vihang Errunza. "Foreign Portfolio Investment in Emerging Securities Markets," *Columbia Journal of World Business* (1982), 35–63.

Ajami, Riad, and Dara Khambata. *International Debts and Lending: Structure and Policy Responses*. Columbus, Ohio: Publishing Horizons, 1986.

Anatomy of World Markets. London: Goldman Sachs, September 1988.

Anckonie, Alex III. "Domestic Financial Intermediation in Developing Countries: What Can the Private Sector Accomplish?" Unpublished manuscript, May 1983.

____. "A Quadratic Program for Determining Efficient Frontier Portfolio Compositions Using the Sas Language," *1985 SUGI Proceedings*. Cary, N.C.: SAS Institute, 55–60.

Anckonie, Alex III, and Chang-hyun Chi, "Internationalization of the Korean Stock Market," paper presented at the Korea Economic Institute of America Meeting, November 5, 1986.

____. "Internationalization of the Korean Stock Market," unpublished manuscript, George Washington University, June 1986.

Anckonie, Alex III, and Nadia El-Abbassy. "Estimating the Expected Variance-Covariance Matrix in the International Financial Portfolio Asset Allocation Problem." Monograph Number 86-2. Washington, D.C.: George Washington University, July 1986.

Arowolo, E. A. "The Development of Capital Markets in Africa, with Particular Reference to Kenya and Nigeria." *IMF Staff Paper*, July 1971.

Aylen, Jonathan. "Privatization in Developing Countries," *Lloyds Bank Review* (January 1987), 15–30.

Basseer, Potkin. "The Role of Financial Intermediation in Economic Development: The Case of Iran 1888–1978." D.B.A. Dissertation. George Washington University, July 13, 1982.

Ben-Bassat, Avraham. "Optimal Composition of Foreign Exchange Reserves," *Journal of International Economics* (May 1980), 285–95.

Bergstrom, Gary L. "A New Route to Higher Returns and Lower Risks," *Journal of Portfolio Management* (Autumn 1975), 30–38.

Bhatt, V.V. "On Financial Innovations and Credit Market Evolution," *Economic and Political Weekly* 20 (November 2, 1985): 1889–91.

Bhatt, V. V., and Alan R. Roe. "Capital Market Imperfections and Economic Development." World Bank Staff Working Paper No. 338, 1979.

Birinyi, Laszlo, and Johnson M. Donora. *Emerging and Secondary Equity Markets: An Introduction*. Salomon Brothers, Inc., June 1988.

Black, F. "International Capital Market Equilibrium with Investment Barriers," *Journal of Financial Economics* 1 (1974): 337–52.

Black, Harold, William Darity, and Bobbie Lee Horn. "Financial Intermediation and Economic Development: A Survey of Theoretical and Empirical Work and Policy

Issues." World Bank, Country Policy Department, Background Paper No. 1985-1, 1985.

Brinson, Gary P., and Nimrod Fachler. "Measuring Non–U.S. Equity Performance," *The Journal of Portfolio Management* (Spring 1985), 73–76.

Buffie, E. "Financial Repression, the Structuralists and Stabilization Policy in Semi-Industrialized Economies," *Journal of Development Economics* 14 (1984): 305–22.

Caballero, Thalia, and Roberto Fernandez. "Gains from Diversification in Emerging Capital Markets: The Mexican Experience." Paper presented for Seminar in Finance, American University, 1983.

Calamanti, Andrea. *The Securities Market and Underdevelopment: The Stock Exchange in the Ivory Coast, Morocco and Tunisia.* Milan: Finafrica Giuffra, 1983.

Cameron, Rondo, ed. *Banking and Economic Development.* New York: Oxford University Press, 1972.

Capel, James. *The World of Emerging Markets 1988.* London: James Capel House, June 1988.

Capital Markets: Mobilizing Resources for Development, Washington, D.C.: IFC, Capital Markets Department, 1986, 1988.

Carey, Kenneth. "Nonrandom Price Changes in Association with Trading in Large Block: Evidence of Market Efficiency in Behavior of Investor Returns," *Journal of Business* 50 (1977): 407–14.

Cheng, Hang-Sheng. "Financial Deepening in Pacific Basin Countries," *Economic Review.* Federal Reserve Bank of San Francisco, Summer 1980.

Cho, Yoon Je. "Inefficiencies from Financial Liberalization in the Absence of Well-Functioning Equity Markets," *Journal of Money, Credit and Banking* (May 1986).

_____. "On the Liberalization of the Financial System and Efficiency of Capital Allocation under Uncertainty." Ph.D. Dissertation. Stanford University, 1984.

Copeland, Thomas E., and J. Fred Weston. *Financial Theory and Corporate Policy.* 2nd ed. Reading, Mass.: Addison-Wesley, 1983.

Cuddington, John T. "Capital Flight: Estimates, Issues, and Explanations." World Bank, CDP Discussion Paper No. 1985–51, November 1, 1985.

Dawson, S. M. "The Trend toward Efficiency for Less Developed Stock Exchanges:

Hong Kong," *Journal of Business Finance and Accounting* (Summer 1984), 151–61.

Diaz-Alejandro, Carlos. "Good-bye Financial Repression, Hello Financial Crash," *Journal of Development Economics* 19 (January 1985): 1–24.

Dickie, Robert. "Development of Third World Securities Markets: An Analysis of General Principles and a Case Study of the Indonesian Market," *Law and Policy in International Business* 13 (1981): 177–222.

Drake, P. J. *Money Finance and Development.* New York: John Wiley & Sons, 1980.

____. "Securities Markets in Less-Developed Countries," *Journal of Development Studies* 13 (January 1977): 72–91.

____. "Some Reflections on Problems Affecting Securities Markets in Less Developed Countries," *Savings and Development* 9 (1985): 5–15.

Eaker, Mark R. "The Numeraire Problem and Foreign Exchange Risk," *Journal of Finance* 36 (May 1981): 419–26.

Edwards, Sebastian. "The Order of Liberalization of the Balance of Payments — Should the Current Account Be Opened up First?" World Bank Staff Working Paper No. 710, 1984.

____. "The Order of Liberalization of the External Sector in Developing Countries." *Essays in International Finance,* No. 156. Princeton: Princeton University Press, December 1984.

Edwards, Sebastian, and Mohsin S. Khan. "Interest Rates in Developing Countries," *Finance and Development* (June 1985), 28–31.

Edwards, Sebastian, and Sweder van Wijnbergen. "The Welfare Effects of Trade and Capital Market Liberalization," *International Economic Review* 27 (February 1986): 141–48.

Elton, E. J., and M. J. Gruber. *International Capital Markets.* New York: North-Holland, 1975.

____. *Modern Portfolio Theory and Investment Analysis.* New York: John Wiley & Sons, 1981.

Emerging Stock Markets Factbook 1988, Washington, D.C.: IFC, Capital Market Department, 1988.

Errunza, Vihang. "Efficiency and the Programs to Develop Capital Markets: The Brazilian Experience," *Journal of Banking and Finance* 3 (1979): 355–82.

____. "Emerging Markets: A New Opportunity for Improving Global Portfolio Performance," *Financial Analysts Journal* (September-October 1983), 51–58.

____. "Gains from Portfolio Diversification into Less Developed Countries' Securities," *Journal of International Business Studies* (Fall/Winter, 1977), 83–99.

____. "Gains from Portfolio Diversification into Less Developed Countries' Securities: A Reply," *Journal of International Business Studies* (Spring/Summer, 1978), 117–23.

____. "On Benefits of Tapping Foreign Portfolio Investments: An Indian Perspective," *Economic and Political Weekly* 21 (February 22, 1986): m17–m19.

____. "On Riskiness of Emerging Markets: Myths and Perceptions versus Theory and Evidence," *Journal of Portfolio Management* (Fall 1987), 62–67.

____. "A Test of Integration, Mild Segmentation and Segmentation Hypotheses." Working Paper, McGill University, Montreal, Canada, 1987.

Errunza, Vihang, and Etienne Losq. "The Behavior of Stock Prices on LDC Markets," *Journal of Banking and Finance* 9 (December 1985): 561–75.

____. "International Asset Pricing under Mild Segmentation: Theory and Test," *Journal of Finance* 40 (March 1985): 150–24.

Errunza, Vihang, and P. Padmanabhan. "Further Evidence on the Benefits of Portfolio Investments in Emerging Markets," *Financial Analysts Journal* (July-August 1988): 76–98.

Errunza, Vihang, and R. Rosenberg. "Investment Risk in Developed and Less Developed Countries," *Journal of Financial and Quantitative Analysis* 17 (1982): 741–62.

Eun, Cheol S., and Bruce G. Resnick. "Currency Factor in International Diversification," *Columbia Journal of World Business* (Summer 1985), 45–53.

Fama, Eugene. "Efficient Capital Markets: A Review of Theory and Empirical Work," *Journal of Finance* (May 1970): 383–417.

____. "Efficient Capital Markets: Reply," *Journal of Finance* (March 1976), 143–54.

Fei, John C. H., Gustav Ranis, and Shirley W. Y. Kuo. *Growth with Equity: The Taiwan Case.* Oxford University Press, 1979.

"Financial Innovations and Debt Problems Spur Important Market Changes in Capital Markets," *IMF Survey* (March 31, 1986): 102–6.

"Financial Intermediation." World Bank Policy Paper, INDFD, February 1985a.

Fraga, Javier Gonzalez. "The Impact of Inflation on Securities Markets," in Bruck, Nicholas, ed. *Capital Markets under Inflation* (Buenos Aires: Stock Exchange of Buenos Aires, Argentina, 1982), 339.

Francis, Jack, and Stephen Archer. *Portfolio Analysis.* Englewood Cliffs, N.J.: Prentice-Hall, 1979.

Freeman, Andrew. "Emerging Markets," *Global Investor* (May 1987), 27–51.

Friedland, Jonathan. "Will Anyone Bet on Third-World Stocks?" *Institutional Investor* (July 1985), 155–58.

Fritz, R. G. "Time Series Evidence of the Causal Relationship between Financial Deepening and Economic Development," *Journal of Economic Development* (July 1984), 91–111.

Fry, Maxwell. "Inflation and Monetary Policy in Hong Kong, Indonesia, Korea, Malaysia, Philippines, Singapore, Taiwan, and Thailand, 1960–1982." Paper presented at the Conference on Inflation in East Asian Countries, Chung Hua Institution for Economic Research, Taiwan, 1983.

_____. "Models of Financially Repressed Developing Economies," *World Development* 120 (1982): 731–50.

_____. "National Saving, Financial Saving and Interest Rate Policy in 14 Asian Developing Economies." Paper presented at the UN International Symposium on the Mobilization of Personal Saving in Developing Countries, Yaounde, Cameroon, December 10–15, 1984.

_____. "Money and Capital or Financial Deepening in Economic Development." *Journal of Money, Credit and Banking* (1978), 464–75.

Galbis, Vincente. "Financial Intermediation and Economic Growth in Less-Developed Countries: A Theoretical Approach," *The Journal of Development Studies* 13 (1977), 58–73.

Gandhi, Devinder K., Anthony Saunders, and Richard S. Woodward. "Thin Capital Markets: A Case Study of the Kuwaiti Stock Market," *Applied Economics* 12 (1980): 341–49.

Gates, Jeffrey. "High Road to Economic Justice: U.S. Encouragement of Employee Stock Ownership Plans in Central America and the Caribbean." Report to the President and the Congress by the Presidential Task Force on Project Economic Justice, October 1986.

Ghanem, Hafez. "Financial Intermediation and Economic Development: A Survey of Theoretical and Empirical Work and Policy Issues." World Bank Background Paper CPDRM 1985-1, November 1985.

Ghanem, Hafez, and Robert Myers. "Country Policies for the Mobilization and Use of Private Financial Savings." World Bank, Resource Mobilization Division, December 1985.

Ghanem, Hafez, and Uri Ben-Zion. "Financial Reform in an Economy with Fragmented Markets." World Bank Discussion Paper, CDP 1985-50, October 1985.

Gill, David. "Development Banks and the Mobilization of Financial Resources." International Finance Corporation (IFC), Capital Markets Department, October 1979.

_____. "Financial System Development and Intermediation Costs." IFC, Capital Markets Department, June 1983.

_____. "Fiscal Policies for the Development of Equity Markets." International Finance Corporation, Korea Investment Finance Corporation Tenth Anniversary Symposium on Capital Markets, June 1981.

_____. "Furthering Securities Market Development." Paper presented to the Eleventh Annual Conference of the International Association of Securities Commissions and Similar Organizations, Paris, France, July 15–16, 1986.

_____. "Implication of Alternative Financial Systems for Securities Market Development." IFC, Capital Markets Department, April 1981.

_____. "The Interdependence of National Securities Markets." Capital Markets Department, Washington, D.C.: IFC, 1984.

_____. "International Investment Opportunities — Emerging Equity Markets in Newly Industrialized Countries." IFC, Capital Markets Department, May 21, 1986.

_____. "Internationalizing the Nigerian Securities Market." Speech presented at the Commemorative Lecture for the 25th Anniversary of the Nigerian Stock Exchange, Lagos, Nigeria, November 19, 1986.

_____. "The Potential for Foreign Portfolio Investment in Emerging Stock Markets." IFC, Templeton Investment Counsel, November 1984.

_____. "Privatization: Opportunities for Financial Market Development." Speech at the Conference on Privatization, Buenos Aires, April 27, 1987.

_____. "Securities Commissions as Developmental Agencies." Speech presented at the Seventh Interamerican Conference of Securities Commissions and Similar Organizations, Washington, D.C., May 24–28, 1982.

_____. "Securities Markets Structural Issues and Challenges." IFC, Capital Markets Department, September 1983.

_____. "Selected Indicators of Financial System Depth 1977, 1980 and 1983." IFC Capital Markets Department, Washington, D.C.: IFC, 1984.

_____. "Some Thoughts on the Implications of Different Financial Institutional Structures on Securities Market Development." International Finance Corporation, Las Instituciones Financieral en el Mercado De Capitales en Chile, December 1979.

_____. "Successes and Failures of Capital Market Development Programs." Paper presented at the Take-off Time for Thailand's Capital Market, Bangkok, Thailand, November 28–29, 1984.

Goldsmith, Raymond W. *Financial Structure and Development*. New Haven: Yale University Press, 1969.

_____. "Capital Markets and Economic Development." Paper presented to the International Symposium on the Development of Capital Markets, Rio de Janeiro, September 1971.

_____. *The Financial Development of India, Japan, and the United States*. New Haven: Yale University Press, 1983.

_____. "The Quantitative International Comparison of Financial Structure and Development," *Journal of Economic History* (March 1975), 216–37.

Goldstein, Carl. "Turning the Capital Tide: Taiwan Seeks Outlets for Its Burgeoning Reserves," *Far Eastern Economic Review* (January 23, 1986), 46–47.

Gropper, Diane Hal. "Mining the Market's Inefficiencies," *Institutional Investor* (July 1985), 81–94.

Gupta, Kanhaya L. *Finance and Economic Growth in Developing Countries*. London: Croom Helm, 1984.

Gurley, John G., and E. S. Shaw. "Financial Structure and Economic Development," *Economic Development and Cultural Change* (April 1967), 257–68.

Hakim, Jonathan R., ed. *Investment Banking and Development Banking*. Washington, D.C.: International Finance Corporation Occasional Paper, 1985.

_____. *Securities Markets*. Washington, D.C.: International Finance Corporation Occasional Paper, 1985.

Hawawini, Gabriel. *European Equity Markets: Price Behavior and Efficiency*. The Monograph Series in Finance and Economics. New York; New York University, 1985.

Hildeburn, Charles G., ed. *The GT Guide to World Equity Markets*. London: Euromoney Publications, 1985.

Hirshleifer, J. *Investment, Interest, and Capital*. Englewood Cliffs, N.J.: Prentice-Hall, 1970.

Ibbotson, Roger G., Richard C. Carr, and Anthony W. Robinson. "International Equity and Bond Returns," *Financial Analysts Journal* (July-August 1982), 61–83.

"IFC Fund Underlines Opportunities in Emerging Securities Markets," *Asian Finance* (February 5, 1986), 38–39.

International Capital Markets: Developments and Prospects. Occasional Paper #43. Washington, D.C.: International Monetary Fund, February 1986.

International Finance Corporation. *Capital Markets: Mobilizing Resources for Development*. Washington, D.C.: IFC, 1986.

International Finance Corporation Annual Reports. Washington, D.C.: World Bank, 1985–1987.

International Financial Statistics. Washington, D.C.: International Monetary Fund, various issues.

Jao, Y. C. "Financial Deepening and Economic Growth: A Cross Section Analysis," *The Malayan Economic Review* (June 1976), 47–57.

John, Kose, Ashok Khanna, and Anthony Saunders. "Allocation Efficiency of the U.S. Stock Market: Theory and Empirical Evidence." Paper prepared for the Capital Markets Department, 1983.

Jung, Woo S. "Financial Development and Economic Growth: International Evidence," *Economic Development and Cultural Change* (January 1986), 333–46.

Kapus, Basant. "Optimal Financial and Foreign Exchange Liberalization of Less Developed Countries," *Quarterly Journal of Economics* 48 (1983).

Kassem, Omar. "Free the Markets and Develop," *Euromoney* (May 1983), 136–47.

Kemp, Lynette J. *The Wardley Guide to World Money and Securities Markets*. London: Euromoney Publications, 1984.

Keynes, John Maynard. *The General Theory of Employment, Interest and Money.* New York: Harcourt Brace, 1936.

Kingdom of Saudi Arabia, Third Development Plan, 1980–1985 A.D. Riyadh, Saudi Arabia: Ministry of Planning, 1980.

Kitchen, Richard L. *Finance for the Developing Country.* Chichester, England: John Wiley & Sons, 1986.

Kraus, Alan, and Hans R. Stoll. "Price Impacts of Block Trading on the New York Stock Exchange," *Journal of Finance* 27 (1972): 569–88.

Laurence, Martin M. "Some Efficiency Characteristics of the Kuala Lumpur and Singapore Stock Markets." Paper presented to the Financial Management Association Annual Meeting, October 22–24, 1981, Cincinnati, Ohio.

Lease, R. C., and W. G. Lewellan. "Market Efficiency across Securities Exchanges," *Journal of Economics and Business* (1982), 101–9.

Lee, S. Y., and Y. C. Jao. *Financial Structure and Monetary Policies in Southeast Asia.* New York: St. Martin's Press, 1982.

Legarda, Benito. "Philosophy of Financial Market Building," Washington, D.C.: International Finance Corporation Discussion Paper, August 1986.

Lessard, Donald R. "International Portfolio Diversification: A Multivariate Analysis for a Group of Latin American Countries," *Journal of Finance* (1973), 619–33.

____. "International Financing for Developing Countries: The Unfulfilled Promise." World Bank Staff Working Paper No. 783, 1986.

____. "World, Country and Industry Relationships in Equity Returns: Implications for Risk Reduction Through International Diversifications," *Financial Analyst Journal* (January-February 1976): 2–8.

____. "World, National and Industry Factors in Equity Returns," *Journal of Finance* 29 (May 1974): 379–91.

Lessard, Donald R., and John Williamson. *Financial Intermediation beyond the Debt Crisis.* Washington, D.C.: Institute for International Economics, September 1985.

Levy, Haim, and Marshall Sarnat. "Devaluation Risk and the Portfolio Analysis of International Investment." In Elton and Gruber. *International Capital Market.* New York: North-Holland, 1975, 177–206.

Lowe, John W. "Financial Markets in Developing Countries," *Finance and Development* (December 1974), 38–41.

Long, M. "Review of Financial Sector Work." World Bank, INDFD, October 30, 1983.

Makin, Claire. "Wall Street's Electronic Cops," *Institutional Investor* (February 1986), 69–71.

Markowitz, Harry. "Portfolio Selection," *Journal of Finance* 7 (March 1952): 77–91.

____. *Portfolio Selection: Efficient Diversification of Investment.* New Haven: Yale University Press, 1959.

Massmann, Juan Ricardo. "Liquidity Premium in the Chilean Stock Market Exchange." Paper presented to the Business Association of Latin American Studies, Washington, D.C., 1985.

Mayshar, Joram. "On Divergence of Opinion and Imperfections in Capital Markets," *The American Economic Review* 73 (March 1983): 114–28.

McKinno, Ronald I. "Financial Repression and the Liberalization Problem within Less Developed Countries." In S. Grassman and E. Lundberg, eds. *The World Economic Order: Past and Prospects.* New York: St. Martin's Press, 1981.

____. "How to Manage a Repressed Economy." *Essays in International Finance.* Princeton: Princeton University Press, 1981.

____. *Money and Capital in Economic Development.* Washington, D.C.: Brookings Institution, 1973.

____. "The Order of Economic Liberalization: Lessons from Chile and Argentina," *Carnegie-Rochester Conference Series on Public Policy* 17 (1982): 159–86.

Mohareb, Nabil S. "Policy Measures for Development of Money and Capital Markets," *Middle East Executive Reports* (May 1986), 8–20.

Musich, Arnaldo T. "Inflation in Brazil," comment on paper by Jorje Del Canto, "Impact of Inflation on the Development of Capital Markets in Argentina and Brazil," in Bruck, Nicholas, ed. *Capital Markets* 187.

Myers, Robert, and S. Sriram. "Cross-Country Financial Relationships." World Bank CPD, December 1985.

Papaioannou, George J. "Thinness and Short-Run Price Dependence in the Athens Stock Exchange," *Greek Economic Review* (1982), 315–33.

Park, Yoon S., and Jack Zwick. *International Banking in Theory and Practice*. Menlo Park, Calif.: Addison-Wesley, 1985.

Patrick, H. T. "Financial Development and Economic Growth in Underdeveloped Countries," *Economic Development and Cultural Change* (January 1966), 174–89.

Pearson, Peter. "Foreign Investment Funds from an International Investor's Viewpoint: Commentator Remarks." *Capital Market Development in the Asia-Pacific Region*. Philippines: Asian Development Bank, 1986.

____. "The Promotion of the Banking Habit and Economic Development," *Journal of Development Studies* (July 1966).

Quarterly Review of Emerging Stock Markets, 3rd Quarter 1988. Washington, D.C.: IFC, Capital Markets Department, 1988.

Rohrer, Julie. "Ferment in Academia," *Institutional Investor* (July 1985), 69–78.

Rowley, Anthony. "Capitalism's Comeback: Asian Developing Countries Become More Market-Oriented," *Far Eastern Economic Review* 30 (January 1986): 44–46.

Rybczynski, T. M. "The Internationalization of the Financial System and the Developing Countries: The Evolving Relationship." World Bank Staff Working Paper No. 788, 1986.

Saini, Krishnan G. "Capital Market Innovations and Financial Flows to Developing Countries." World Bank Staff Working Paper No. 784, 1986.

Salice, Licia, and Robert Myers. "Financial Savings in Developing Countries: A Review of Financial Sector Work and Its Policy Implications." World Bank Discussion Paper, CDP 1985–44, October 1985.

Sametz, Arnold W. *Financial Development and Economic Growth: The Consequences of Underdeveloped Capital Markets*. New York: New York University Press, 1972.

Samuels, J. M., and N. Yacout. "Stock Exchanges in Developing Countries," *Savings and Development* 4 (1981): 217–30.

Scholes, Myron. "The Market for Securities: Substitution versus Price Pressure and the Effects of Information on Share Prices," *Journal of Business* 45 (1972): 179–211.

Schumpeter, J. A. *The Theory of Economic Development*. Cambridge, Mass.: Harvard University Press, 1954.

Shaked, I. "International Equity Markets and the Investment Horizon." *Journal of Portfolio Management* (Winter 1985): 80–84.

Sharma, J. L. "Efficient Capital Markets and Random Character of Stock Price Behavior in a Developing Economy," *The Indian Economic Journal* 31 (October-December 1983): 53–68.

Sharma, J., and R. Kennedy. "A Comparative Analysis of Stock Price Behavior on the Bombay, London and New York Exchanges," *Journal of Financial and Quantitative Analysis* (September 1977), 391–414.

Shaw, Edward S. *Financial Deepening in Economic Development.* New York: Oxford University Press, 1973.

Skully, Michael T. *Merchant Banking in ASEAN: A Regional Examination of Its Development and Operations.* Kuala Lumpur: Oxford University Press, 1983.

____, ed. *Financial Institutions and Markets in Southeast Asia: A Study of Brunei, Indonesia, Malaysia, Philippines, Singapore and Thailand.* London: Macmillan, 1984.

Smith, Gordon W., and John T. Cuddington, eds. *International Debt and the Developing Countries.* Washington, D.C.: World Bank, 1985.

Smith, Paul F. *Comparative Financial Systems.* New York: Praeger, 1982.

Solis, Raul, and Alberto Usobiaga. "Returns, Efficiency and Diversification in the Mexican Stock Market." Paper presented at the Academy of International Business Annual Meeting, New Orleans, October 1980.

Solnik, Bruno H. "The Advantages of Domestic and International Diversification." In Elton and Gruber. *International Capital Markets,* 165–76.

____. "The International Pricing of Risk: An Empirical Investigation of the World Capital Market Structure," *Journal of Finance* 29 (1974): 365–78.

____. "Note on the Validity of the Random Walk for European Stock Prices." *Journal of Finance* (December 1973), 1151–59.

____. "Why Not Diversify Internationally Rather than Domestically?" *Financial Analyst Journal* (July-August 1974): 48–54.

____. "Testing International Asset Pricing: Some Pessimistic Views," *The Journal of Finance* 32 (May 1977), 503–12.

Solnik, Bruno H., and Bernard Noetzlin. "Optimal International Asset Allocation," *Journal of Portfolio Management* (Fall 1982), 11–21.

Stapleton, Richard C., and Marti G. Subrahmanyam. "Market Imperfections, Capital Market Equilibrium, and Corporate Finance," *Journal of Finance* 32 (May 1977): 307–19.

Stiglitz, J. E., and Andrew Weiss. "Incentive Effects of Terminations," *American Economic Review* 73 (December 1983): 913–27.

Stonehill, Arthur I., and Kare B. Dullum. *Internationalizing the Cost of Capital: The Novo Experience and National Policy Implications.* New York: John Wiley & Sons, 1982.

Stultz, R. "A Model of International Asset Pricing," *Journal of Financial Economics* 9 (1981): 383–403.

____. "On the Effects of Barriers to International Investment," *Journal of Finance* 36 (September 1981): 923–34.

Subrahmanyam, Marti G. "On the Optimality of International Capital Market Integration," *Journal of Financial Economics* 2 (March 1975): 3–28.

Sudweeks, Bryan L. "Equity Market Development in Developing Countries: General Principles, Case Studies, Portfolio Implications, and Relevance for the People's Republic of China." Ph.D. Dissertation. George Washington University, Washington, D.C., March 1987.

____. "Financial Development and Securities Markets in Economic Development." Paper presented to the Washington, D.C. Consortium of Business Faculty, April 17, 1986.

Sudweeks, Bryan, and Alex Anckonie III. "Portfolio Implications of Investing in Developing Countries." Paper presented at the 1987 AIB Conference, Chicago, November 1987.

Sudweeks, Bryan, and Phillip Grub. "Securities Markets and the People's Republic of China," *Journal of Economic Development* 13 (June 1988): 51–69.

Sudweeks, Bryan, and Brent Tanner. "International Venture Capital: The Case of Korea, China and the Philippines." Unpublished manuscript, December 1984.

Tinaikar, Durgesh. "LDC Companies and Euroequity Markets." Washington, D.C.: Capital Markets Department, International Finance Corporation, October 21, 1986.

Tobin, James. "Liquidity Preference as Behavior toward Risk," *Review of Economics and Statistics* 26 (February 1958): 65–86.

____. "On the Efficiency of the Financial System," *Lloyds Bank Review* 153 (July 1984): 1–15.

Uthaisri and Vachratith. "New Life for Corporations," *Asian Finance* (September 15, 1979): 80.

Virmani, Arvind. "Government Policy and the Development of Financial Markets." World Bank Staff Working Paper No. 747, 1985.

Wai, U. Tun. "The Role of Unorganized Financial Markets in Economic Development and in the Formulation of Monetary Policy." IMF Institute, February 5, 1977.

Wai, U. Tun, and Hugh T. Patrick. "Stock and Bond Issues and Capital Markets in Less Developed Countries," *IMF Staff Papers* 20 (July 1973): 253–317.

Wall, Peter. "Venture Capital Activities in Selected Countries." IFC, Capital Markets Department, July 1986.

Warfield, Gerald. *How to Buy Foreign Stocks and Bonds.* New York: Harper & Row, 1985.

Wilson, J. S. G. "The Art of Developing a Capital Market." In C. R. Whittlesey and J. S. C. Wilson, eds. *Essays in Money and Banking in Honor of R. S. Sayers.* Oxford: Clarendon Press, 1968.

Yassukovich, Stanislas. "Euro-Equities Are Here to Stay." *Euromoney* (May 1984), 70.

Yotopoulos, P. A., and J. B. Nugent. *The Economics of Development: Empirical Investigations.* New York: McGraw-Hill, 1978.

Yusaf, Shahid, and R. Kyle Peters. "Capital Accumulation and Economic Growth." World Bank Staff Working Paper No. 712, 1985.

Index

About the Author

Bryan L. Sudweeks is responsible for investment strategy, research, and trading in Asia, Greece, Jordan, Kenya and Zimbabwe at Emerging Markets Investors Corporation (EMIC), a Washington D.C.–based investment management firm. EMIC specializes in investing in the emerging equity markets of newly industrializing countries in Asia, Latin America, the Mid-East, Southern Europe and Africa. Formerly, Dr. Sudweeks served as consultant to the Capital Markets Department of the International Finance Corporation (World Bank), Visiting Assistant Professor of International Business Administration at George Washington University, and financial analyst with Amdahl Corporation and Utah International, Inc.

Dr. Sudweeks received his Ph.D. from George Washington University and his M.B.A. and B.A. from Brigham Young University.